VIOLENCE AGAINST WOMEN

VIOLENCE AGAINST WOMEN

Myths, Facts, Controversies

Walter S. DeKeseredy

University of Toronto Press

LIBRARY AND ARCHIVES CANADA CATALOGUING IN PUBLICATION

DeKeseredy, Walter S., 1959–
Violence against women : myths, facts, controversies / Walter S. DeKeseredy.

Includes bibliographical references and index.
Also available in electronic formats.
ISBN 978-1-4426-0399-8

1. Women—Violence against—Canada.   2. Women—Violence
against.   3. Abused women—Psychology.   4. Violence in men.   I. Title.

HV6250.4.W65D428 2011   362.88082'0971   C2010-907395-9

We welcome comments and suggestions regarding any aspect of our
publications—please feel free to contact us at news@utphighereducation.com
or visit our Internet site at www.utppublishing.com.

North America
5201 Dufferin Street
North York, Ontario,
Canada, M3H 5T8

2250 Military Road
Tonawanda, New York,
USA, 14150

UK, Ireland, and continental Europe
NBN International
Estover Road, Plymouth, PL6 7PY, UK
ORDERS PHONE: 44 (0) 1752 202301
ORDERS FAX: 44 (0) 1752 202333
ORDERS E-MAIL:
enquiries@nbninternational.com

ORDERS PHONE: 1-800-565-9523
ORDERS FAX: 1-800-221-9985
ORDERS E-MAIL: utpbooks@utpress.utoronto.ca

The University of Toronto Press acknowledges the financial support for its
publishing activities of the Government of Canada through the Canada
Book Fund.

Printed in Canada

Book design by Zack Taylor, Metapolis.

This book is dedicated to my mother, Eva Jantz.

Contents

Preface

About three years ago, a colleague suggested I write a new book on violence against women in Canada. I questioned the need for another book on the abuse of women in private places and in intimate relationships. After all, since the late 1970s, many books on various types of male-to-female violence have been published. However, since Canadian scholars, practitioners, and activists are constantly generating new empirical, theoretical, and political ways of understanding sexual assaults, wife beating, femicide, and the like, I decided it was indeed time to write an overview of their work. *Violence Against Women: Myths, Facts, Controversies* also includes some important contributions made by authors in other countries, especially those based in the United States, the United Kingdom, and Australia.

Chapter One describes and evaluates narrow and broad definitions of violence against women. Certainly, defining male-to-female violence is subject to much debate. Chapter Two focuses on the amount of violence Canadian women experience in current or former intimate relationships. A key point made there is that acts of violence are not rare incidents and in fact can happen to any woman. Further, contrary to popular belief, women are much safer on the streets than they are behind closed doors.

Preface

Due in large part to the efforts of fathers' rights groups, conservative journalists and politicians, and others with a vested interest in challenging the gains made by women over the last 30 years, many Canadians believe that women are as violent as men in intimate relationships. It may be painfully obvious but worth stating again: nothing can be further from the truth. The purpose, then, of Chapter Three is to challenge the widely held notion that intimate violence is a gender-neutral problem.

Chapter Four provides sociological answers to the question "Why does he do that?," the title of Lundy Bancroft's best selling US trade book on angry and controlling men. This chapter also demonstrates that most men who physically, sexually, and psychologically attack women are not "sick." Rather, they are motivated by sociological and social psychological forces, such as peer-group membership, pornographic media, and both familial and societal patriarchy.

Perhaps the most commonly asked question about abuse in intimate relationships is why women just don't get up and leave. The reality is that most abused women *do* leave, but some are trapped in violent relationships with no way out. Research included in Chapter Five compels Canadians to ask "what keeps her from leaving" rather than "why does she stay."

A key objective of Chapter Six is to show that while many Canadians may not have directly experienced violence against women, they still suffer from its effects. In addition to focusing on the damage done to women and their children, data on the broader economic costs of beatings, homicides, rapes, and so on are presented.

As Jackson Katz puts it in Chapter Nine of his book *The Macho Paradox: Why Some Men Hurt Women and How All Men Can Help*, "It takes a village to rape a woman." Heavily influenced by this empirically informed observation, Chapter Seven points out that we need to develop and implement short- and long-term policies that focus on broader social forces that contribute to violence against women and that relying solely on the criminal justice system to solve violence is highly problematic.

Years ago, historians used to teach their students to "tell a story." This phrase is now out of fashion because it does not convey the years that historians spend accumulating the facts behind the story. Yet the heritage remains, and many historians tell vivid and interesting "stories" about their topics. Social scientists, on the other hand, are all too often attacked for being pedantic and boring, concerned more about impressing each other with their footnotes and citations than with their research topics. I attempt to tell the story of woman abuse in Canada in this book without ever losing sight of the empirical, theoretical, and political content that needs to be presented intelligibly to an interested audience. For example, whenever possible, I provide real-life stories and anecdotes to illustrate complex issues. Sometimes, the anecdotes will be about my own experiences as a man, as a researcher, and as an activist.

While being as fair as possible, this is not a "value-free" book. For one thing, with its decidedly sociological orientation, it sees a much smaller role for biological and psychological perspectives on woman abuse. For another, it gives room to research, theories, and policies that are often ignored or poorly treated by the mainstream media, politicians, and the general public. *Violence Against Women* was written with the intent that it will play a role in the ongoing struggle to end much of the pain and suffering experienced by thousands of Canadian women on a daily basis.

Acknowledgements

Like any book, this one is a product of collective effort. I am deeply grateful for the support, encouragement, and advice provided by University of Toronto Press editor Anne Brackenbury and my copy editor, Betsy Struthers. Others also deserve special recognition. As has been the case since I started my career as a young sociologist, I have greatly benefited from the comments, criticisms, lessons, emotional support, and influences provided by these friends and colleagues: Bernie Auchter, Karen Bachar, Gregg Barak, Carol Barkwell, Ola Barnett, Raquel Kennedy Bergen, Helene Berman, Rebecca Block, Douglas Brownridge, Susan Caringella, Meda Chesney-Lind, Kimberly J. Cook, Colleen Dell, Joseph F. Donnermeyer, Molly Dragiewicz, Desmond Ellis, Rus Funk, Alberto Godenzi, Judith Grant, Barbara Hart, Peter Jaffe, Yasmin Jiwani, Holly Johnson, David Kauzlarich, Penny Krowitz, Sally Laskey, Julian Lo, Linda MacLeod, Barbara MacQuarrie, Raymond J. Michalowski, Susan L. Miller, Louise Moyer, Steven L. Muzzatti, Patrik Olsson, Tony Porter, Lori Post, Claire M. Renzetti, Robin Robinson, Martin D. Schwartz, Aysan Sev'er, Cynthia Simpson, the late Michael D. Smith, Betsy Stanko, Cris Sullivan, and Kenneth D. Tunnell.

Of course, *Violence Against Women* came to fruition with the help of Pat and Andrea DeKeseredy and Eva Jantz. One of my "fur children," Ola B. (named after feminist psychologist

Acknowledgements

Ola Barnett) also warrants special thanks here for reminding me that cats, too, can be a source of much support. She was 22 years old at the time of completing this book and has sat next to my keyboard ever since she joined our family.

ONE

What is Violence Against Women?[1]

It is crucial...that researchers examine the assumptions and biases underlying the terms they use, as well as the ways in which these terms constrain their results and conclusions. This is particularly crucial in fields that use popular terms likely to be influenced by the unacknowledged biases and political concerns of the dominant group.[2]

When the term *crime victim* comes up in the course of daily conversations with friends, relatives, acquaintances, university peers, and professors, it generally refers to a person harmed by a violent predatory stranger on the street or in some other public place, such as a club or a bar. However, knowingly or unknowingly, all of us have been, or will be, victimized by one or more highly injurious behaviours that commonly escape the purview of criminal law. As University of San Francisco criminologist Robert Elias put it over 20 years ago:

> We may have a limited social reality of crime and victimization that excludes harms such as consumer fraud, pollution, unnecessary drugs and surgery, food additives, workplace hazards and diseases, police violence, censorship, discrimination, poverty, exploitation, and war. We suffer victimization not only by other individuals, but also by governments and other social institutions, not to mention the psychological victimization bred by our own insecurities.[3]

If these harms are typically not viewed as crimes in the strict sense of the word, the same can be said about the on-ice conduct of some National Hockey League players. One widely publicized event that still remains in the minds of many

---

BOX 1.1 **Canadian Spanking Laws**

A Supreme Court of Canada ruling handed down on January 30, 2004, upholds the "spanking laws" in Canada, but for the first time the high court has issued guidelines that say spanking teenagers or children under age two, hitting a child in the head, or using objects like belts or rulers are actions that go too far.

In a deeply split 6-3 decision, the court ruled...the so-called "spanking" defence in Canadian law does not protect or excuse "outbursts of violence against a child motivated by anger or animated by frustration."

Still, parents, their stand-in caregivers, and teachers may use reasonable force if it is for "educative or corrective purposes," Chief Justice Beverley McLachlin wrote for the majority.

"The reality is," wrote McLachlin, that without such a defence, Canada's "broad assault law would criminalize force falling far short of what we think as corporal punishment, like placing an unwilling child in a chair for a five-minute 'time-out.'"

Source: CanadianLawSite.Com, 2004, p. 3.

Canadians is the vicious attack on March 8, 2004, by Vancouver Canucks player Todd Bertuzzi on the Colorado Avalanche's Steve Moore. From behind, Bertuzzi grabbed Moore's jersey and punched him on the side of his head, an attack that still can be viewed on the video-sharing website YouTube. Following this assault, several members of both teams, including Bertuzzi, jumped on Moore. Not surprisingly, Moore suffered major injuries and will never play professional hockey again. Should those who commit acts like Bertuzzi's be labelled violent criminals? Or are their potentially lethal actions "just part of the game"? Many people obviously agree with this latter statement because Bertuzzi went on to play for Team Canada in the 2006 Winter Olympics in Turin, Italy, and does not have a criminal record.

Only a small number of cases such as the assault on Steve Moore have resulted in litigation. Therefore, it is fair to conclude that despite the life-threatening nature of some

---

BOX 1.2 Study Links Childhood Abuse to Increased Risk of Cancer

Physical childhood abuse appears to be a risk factor for cancer, a University of Toronto study says.

"It really surprised us," researcher Esme Fuller-Thomson said yesterday of the apparent link discerned from statistical analysis.

The study, to be published July 15 in the American Cancer Society journal *Cancer*, does not suggest that physical damage to a child's body leads to cancer.

Rather, it suggests a correlation between psychological damage from childhood physical abuse and an elevated cancer risk in adulthood—a mind-body association that medical science can often be reluctant to explore.

"Social scientists work on one side and medical researchers work on the other," said Fuller-Thomson, an associate professor in the faculty of social work and the department of family and community medicine.

Source: Goddard, 2009, p. A2.

"punch-ups," many Canadians see nothing wrong with "hockey fisticuffs."[4] Similarly many people, including some who belong to the group that the late sociologist C. Wright Mills referred to as the "power elite,"[5] see nothing wrong with slapping or spanking a child. In fact, most Canadians view spanking as legitimate chastisement, and they strongly defend the "right" of parents to raise their children as they see fit even though many physicians, community-based activists, front-line workers, academics, and others. define slapping and spanking children as abusive or violent. Although spanking is the most universal type of physical violence, it is illegal in Sweden, Finland, Denmark, Norway, and Austria,[6] although not in Canada (under certain conditions; see Box 1.1). The research briefly reviewed in Box 1.2 may change your mind about the permissibility of punishing children physically.

A much longer list of hurtful behaviours that many people do not regard as violent could easily be provided here.

We must consider, however, that violence is often "not a quality of the act the person commits, but rather a consequence of the application by others of rules and sanctions to an offender."[7] In other words, violence is a label, and there is nothing automatic about the relation between committing a violent act and being labelled criminal or deviant.[8] The same argument could be made about the topic covered in this book—violence against women in private places.

About 10 years ago, Martin Schwartz and I stated what was obvious to experts in the field: the number of studies on violence against women had increased dramatically.[9] Today, we can easily repeat this observation. Indeed, it is a major challenge to keep up with the empirical and theoretical work on one of the world's most compelling gendered social problems. That the field's leading periodical, *Violence Against Women: An International and Interdisciplinary Journal*, is able to publish monthly is an important statement on the amount of time, money, and effort devoted around the world to enhancing a social-scientific understanding of the myriad ways in which women are harmed by intimate partners.

While new studies are being conducted on a daily basis and new theories are being constructed and tested, one thing we do not have is an agreed-upon firm definition of violence against women. As Dean Kilpatrick, Director of the Medical University of South Carolina's National Crime Victims Research and Treatment Center, correctly points out, the debate about whether to define violence against women narrowly or broadly is "old, fierce, and unlikely to be resolved in the near future."[10] Similarly, there is a major debate surrounding terminology. Many people use language that specifically either names women as the objects of abuse or names men as the perpetrators by employing terms such as "woman abuse," "violence against women," and "male-to-female violence."[11] Others fervently oppose such labels and use such gender-neutral terms as "family violence" or "intimate partner violence" (IPV), often claiming that women are as violent as men in marriage, cohabiting relationships, dating, and other intimate relationships.[12] Their rationale is based on some Canadian national survey data presented in Chapter Three, which, at first glance, show that violence in intimate

4

heterosexual relationships is sex-symmetrical. Some government agencies and community groups favour these labels because they claim that they are more inclusive.[13] Regardless of the reasons why people use gender-neutral terms, such language suggests that violence results from ordinary, everyday social interactions in the family or other intimate relationships that have gone wrong and that women are just as responsible for the problem as men.[14] Since the debate about women's use of violence is addressed in great detail in Chapter Three, the main objective of this chapter is to describe and evaluate narrow and broad definitions.

NARROW VERSUS BROAD DEFINITIONS

Major debates over definition are not trivial; they seriously affect how data are gathered, as well as the quality and quantity of social support services for women who are beaten, sexually assaulted, and abused in other ways by intimates or acquaintances. Further, definitions are used politically as tools in social struggles. Together with poverty, unemployment, terrorism, and other social problems, violence against women is a highly politicized topic of social-scientific inquiry, and definitions of this variation of what feminist scholar Elizabeth Stanko refers to as "intimate intrusions"[15] reflect this reality.

Narrow Definitions

Narrow legal definitions of violence that focus mainly on physical abuse or sexual assaults involving forced penetration are most common. A former Member of Parliament, Roger Gallaway, argued that studies like the Canadian National Survey of Woman Abuse in University/College Dating (CNS) "are distorted even further by a broadening of the concept of abuse."[16] Many political conservatives assert that violence-against-women studies, which simultaneously examine physical and non-physical acts (e.g., psychological, verbal, spiritual, and economic abuse), are ideologically driven and are designed to artificially inflate the rates of woman abuse to make political points.[17]

Comparable criticisms come from some Canadian feminists. In her critique of the CNS, University of Toronto sociologist Bonnie Fox states that "by combining what is debatably abusive with what *everyone* [italics added] agrees to be seriously abusive," the latter becomes trivialized. In fact, Fox views psychological or emotional victimization as "soft-core abuse."[18] Other feminists define psychological assaults as "early warning signs" of physical and sexual attacks, rather than as abusive in and of themselves.[19]

Likewise, as noted in Chapter Three, some researchers, right-wing fathers' rights groups, and other anti-feminists who claim that women are as violent as men do not include in their definitions homicide, stalking, sexual assaults that do not involve physical contact, separation/divorce assault, strangulation, and a host of other harms that thousands of women experience on a daily basis. Recent efforts to promote the use of gender-neutral language selectively cite research to incorrectly characterize violence as bi-directional, mutual, or sex symmetrical. Moreover, those who promote gender-neutral language do not see gender as a major determinant of violence against women. It cannot be emphasized enough that gender is not the same as sex. Rather, as Edwin Schur reminds us, gender refers to "the sociocultural and psychological shaping, patterning, and evaluating of female and male behaviour."[20]

There are some major problems with narrow legalistic definitions. The definition of violence against spouses used in Statistics Canada's 2004 General Social Survey (GSS) was informed by the Canadian Criminal Code, which is why only 7 per cent of the women in the sample reported at least one incident of violence committed by a current or ex-spouse in the previous five years.[21] This figure does not agree with those generated by other studies that used some version of the Conflict Tactics Scale (CTS), discussed in detail in Chapter Three, to measure wife abuse. Except for Statistics Canada's Violence Against Women Survey,[22] all these studies generated much higher incidence rates (percentage of women who were physically abused in the past year) because they were not presented to respondents as crime surveys, as was the case with the 2004 GSS. Generally, these surveys showed that at least 11 per cent of North American women in marital/cohabiting relationships are physically assaulted by their male partners in any 12-month period. Dutton's comparison of rates of intimate partner violence uncovered by crime surveys and non-crime surveys found the latter figures to be six times higher than the former.[23]

Crime surveys create a set of "demand characteristics," and unless respondents clearly label acts as criminal in their own mind, they tend not to report them. If people do not think of their spouse's violence as "criminal," they may not report it in such a survey. In fact, close to 83 per cent of marital violence incidents are not reported in contexts where the research emphasis is on criminal assault and victimization.[24]

There are a number of other reasons why many researchers, advocates, and practitioners worry about low rates uncovered by government surveys such as the 2004 GSS. Perhaps one of the most important is that policy-makers tend to listen only to big numbers. Unfortunately, if government officials are led by some survey researchers using narrow definitions to believe that violence against women is not a statistically significant issue, they are not likely to devote sufficient resources to prevent and control one of Canada's most pressing social problems.[25]

Narrow definitions not only exacerbate the problem of underreporting, but they also trivialize women's feelings and experiences. The most common, narrow definition of sexual assault is restricted to forced penetration of the vagina, anus, or mouth. The September 25, 2007, Ontario case described in Box 1.3 describes another scenario. Eight boys committed acts that were legally considered sexual assault and were charged accordingly by the police; nonetheless, many people, including some conservative Canadian university professors, saw labelling these perpetrators' behaviours as criminal as "definitional stretching."[26] However, just because some people do not define what happened to the victims as serious does not mean the girls experienced the event lightly. Indeed, what happened to these young women generated much pain and suffering.

Another common concern is that narrow definitions restrain abused women from seeking social support. If a female survivor's male partner's brutal conduct does not coincide with what researchers, criminal justice officials, politicians, or the

BOX 1.3 **Eight Boys Charged with Sex Assault on School Grounds: 12- and 13-Year-Old Students Accused of Restraining and Groping Girls; Parents Fear Charges Overblown**

Eight students at Smithfield Middle School in Rexdale have been charged with sexual assault after allegedly restraining and groping four girls on school property after class. The boys are all 12 and 13, and can't be identified under the Youth Criminal Justice Act. The girls are all 13.

All are students at the public school for grades 6, 7, and 8.

The alleged incidents occurred separately over 45 minutes on September 25 during a basketball game on the court behind the school, which is on Mount Olive Dr., near Finch Ave. W. and Kipling Ave.

A surveillance camera in the area and videotape "did play a part of the investigation," said Supt. Ron Taverner of nearby 23 Division.

Taverner declined to discuss what the tape shows or what exactly police and the girls are alleging.

However, Trevor Ludski, superintendent of the Toronto District School Board, said the girls were allegedly restrained and "the boys then touched the girls over their clothing."

But some parents of the accused boys have expressed concern that the criminal charges are a result of actions that may have been blown out of proportion.

Ludski said a vice-principal was watching a school basketball game in the field outside the school when she noticed a female student who appeared to be upset. Police were then called. The board has issued the eight charged students a letter denying them access to school pending the police investigation, said board officials.

They are being assigned lessons to do at home.

Several of the girls have returned to class.

By mid-afternoon yesterday, parents of some of the accused boys were at 23 Division, angry their sons had been held for hours and perplexed at the severity of the charges.

Source: Powell & Brown, 2007, pp. A1, A27.

general public refer to as abuse or violence, she may be left in a "twilight zone" where she knows that she has been abused but cannot define it in a way that would help her.[27] As stated by a rural woman harmed by separation/divorce sexual assault, "I don't sit around and share. I keep it to myself…. I'm not one to sit around and talk about what happened."[28] In a study of rape survivors conducted by Victoria Pitts and Martin Schwartz, all of the women who were encouraged by the "most helpful" peer to self-blame denied that they had been raped, while all of the women who were encouraged to believe that they were not at fault claimed that they had been raped. As Pitts and Schwartz point out, not only do women who deny their rape fail to seek social support, but in most cases society "takes away their right to feel angry about it."[29]

Thus, narrow definitions exacerbate the problem of under-reporting. If people are asked questions based on narrow legal criteria, researchers will elicit data underestimating the amount of abuse experienced by their respondents. Consequently, as the late Michael D. Smith put it, the scientific credibility of an entire survey is "put into jeopardy, for one cannot know if those women who disclosed having been abused are representative of all victims in the sample."[30]

Broad Definitions

Defining violence against women is a basic social-scientific act, and how one defines this problem is one of the most important research decisions that a methodologist will make. This has been particularly debated in the areas of psychological and emotional abuse, which has been found to be just as, if not more, injurious than physical violence.[31] Diane Follingstad and her colleagues found that 72 per cent of their abused female interviewees reported that psychological abuse had a more severe effect on them than did physical abuse.[32] Some, like this woman who participated in a rural Ohio separation/divorce sexual assault study, say that most physical wounds heal, but the damage to their self-respect and ability to relate to others caused by emotional, verbal, and spiritual violence affects every aspect of their lives:

I couldn't care less if I have sex again in my life. I could care less if I ever had another relationship with a man again in my life. Oh, it's scarred me for life. I think it's physically, mentally, well maybe not so much physically, but emotionally has scarred me for life. You know, and that's the reason why I don't socialize myself with people. I isolate myself from people because if I don't, I get panic attacks. And the dreams they, they're never gone. They're never gone. I mean, I don't care how much you try to put it out of your head; the dreams always bring it back, always. I've been in a sleep clinic where they would videotape me sleeping, being in and out of bed, crawling into a corner screaming, "Please don't hurt me, don't shoot me, don't whatever."[33]

Many women are harmed by sexual assaults that do not involve penetration, such as unwanted acts when they were drunk or high, or when they were unable to give consent.[34] Married and cohabiting women can be "blackmailed" into having sex with their partners. Because there is no threat or actual use of force does not mean that such an experience is not terrifying, emotionally scarring, or highly injurious. One of Diana E.H. Russell's pregnant respondents labelled as rape this assault by her first husband:

The worst raping occasion was in the morning I awoke in labour with my first child. The hospital I was booked into was a thirty-minute drive away, and this being the first time I had undergone childbirth, I had no idea of how close I was to giving birth, or what was to happen to me next. I laboured at home for a few hours until perhaps 11:00 a.m., and then said to my ex-husband that I thought we'd better go to the hospital. The pains were acute and I was panicking that I would not be able to bear them. He looked at me and said, "Oh, all right. But we'd better have a screw first, because it'll be a week before you're home again." I couldn't believe it, even of him. "Please, W., take me to the hospital," I begged as another contraction stormed across my body. "Not until we have a screw," he insisted. I wept, I cried, I pleaded, but he wouldn't budge. The pleading went on until midday, by which time I was frantic to get nursing help. He stood adamant with his arms crossed, a smirk on his face, and jiggling the car keys as a bribe. In the end I submitted. It took two minutes, then we dressed and drove down to the hospital. The baby was born five hours later.[35]

Research also shows that many women have unwanted sex "out of obligation"[36] because of ex-partners' threats to fight for sole custody of children or because they are coerced into having sex for other reasons that do not involve the use of, or threats of, force:

Um, I think that our society, um, that, um, this community that we live in and the society we live in is, um, male dominated in general. And so, um, everything from our media to our family and peer experiences influences the way we, the way women view ourselves. I see many, many, many women submitting to men ... submitting to what they, their men want them to be. I had many, many discussions, over a hundred, women saying to me, my boyfriend wants to have sex, but I don't want to have sex, but I am going to do it anyway to please him. And so I consider that unwanted sex, because, yes, these women are consenting, but they don't know any other out. They have no other option. And that is what I find sad. And there is so much peer influence about being cool, about being heterosexual, you know?[37]

Regardless of whether they find non-physical acts of abuse to be more damaging than physical ones, women targeted by intimate interpersonal violence are rarely only victimized by one type of assault. Rather, they typically suffer from a variety of injurious male behaviours that include physical violence, psychological abuse, economic blackmail, the denial of money even if the woman earns a wage, harm to pets or possessions to which she has an attachment, coercive control, or stalking behaviour. Eighty per cent of the 43 rural Ohio women interviewed by me and my colleagues stated that they were victimized by two or more of these forms of abuse.[38] This is yet another key reason why many feminist scholars, activists, and practitioners assert that we should develop and operationalize broad definitions such as this:

> Woman abuse is the misuse of power by a husband, intimate partner (whether male or female), ex-husband, or ex-partner against a woman, resulting in a loss of dignity, control, and safety as well as a feeling of powerlessness and entrapment experienced by the woman who is the direct victim of ongoing or repeated physical, psychological, economic, sexual, verbal, and/or spiritual abuse. Woman abuse also includes persistent threats or forcing women to witness violence against their children, other relatives, friends, pets, and/or cherished possessions by their husbands, partners, ex-husbands, or ex-partners.[39]

Definitions like this are often criticized for including "everything but the kitchen sink." Of course, including too many behaviours under the rubric of violence may result in a breakdown of social exchanges between people as they label each other's actions abusive or violent.[40] Moreover, it is much more difficult to study 50 behaviours at once than to study one or two. Nevertheless, a large number of abused women reject the notion that "sticks and stones may break my bones but words will never hurt me." For reasons offered here and elsewhere, many non-violent, highly injurious behaviours are just as worthy of in-depth empirical, theoretical, and political attention as those that cause physical harm. Furthermore, physical, sexual, economic, and psychological abuse are not mutually exclusive.

Although there is an ongoing anti-feminist backlash against broad definitions of violence, a number of social scientists, government agencies, and university research centres recognize their merits. Despite some methodological problems identified a few years ago with the US National Violence Against Women Survey, it did include measures of stalking, physical violence, sexual assault, and emotionally abusive or controlling behaviours. Statistics Canada's 1993 Violence Against Women Survey also measured a variety of hurtful behaviours, as did the CNS.[41] As noted in Box 1.4, five major research centres and many university-based women's studies programs in Canada

BOX 1.4 Out From the Shadows: Women's Studies Programs Have Changed How We View Violence Against Women

In response to the massacre of 14 female students at the École Polytechnique in 1989, Health Canada and the Social Sciences and Humanities Research Council funded the creation of five research centres to help demystify the violence inflicted on women. The result has been a much more structured approach to knowledge creation in the field, says Genevieve Lessard, director of the Quebec-based Interdisciplinary Research Centre on Family Violence and Violence Against Women.

Carmen Gill, of the Muriel McQueen Fergusson Centre for Research on Family Violence (affiliated with the University of New Brunswick), agrees. She says that on the strength of solid scientific inquiry, the five research centres have not only changed researchers' and policy-makers' perception of the problem, but also have produced tremendous expertise.

Today, violence against women carries a broader definition in scientific circles, and it's studied in the light of previously ignored phenomena or, as Dr. Gill puts it, keeping in mind particular realities, such as the role of colonialism and oppression in the violence exacted on aboriginal women, or the vulnerability of elderly women, pregnant women, or women with disabilities.

This broader look at violence allows women's studies to shed light on different realities or special circumstances that most often go unnoticed in standard police investigations or in general studies.

Now, backed by enough historical perspective to report more accurately on the full scope of violence, the field of women's studies is helping to expand prevention strategies and interventions in line with these different realities.

Source: Kettani, 2009, p. 19.

broadly define violence against women and have influenced how many Canadians view this problem.

A major problem still remains. Despite the trend toward using broad definitions, we still see variance in rates of abuse across studies, even when they use similar measures. This is due to sampling differences, different data-gathering techniques (e.g., telephone interviews vs. computer surveys), and other methodological factors.

SUMMARY

Defining violence against women has been a catalyst for bringing people, including researchers, together. Unfortunately, it has also created bitter divisions among social scientists and others involved in the ongoing struggle to make intimate relationships safer. How do we minimize or overcome these divisions? There are no simple answers to this question, and perhaps there will never be a consensus, despite strong attempts to meet this objective by researchers such as the late Linda Saltzman and her colleagues at the Centers for Disease Control and Prevention in Atlanta.[42]

Although, as described in Box 1.5, researchers typically define violence against women according to their discipline's modes of inquiry, for many women, especially those who are battered, psychologically abused, or sexually assaulted, a key point to consider is whether researchers' definitions are sensitive to their subjective experiences.[43] As British feminist scholar Ruth Hall discovered, just "ask any woman" about her encounters with violence and other types of intimate abuse and you will undoubtedly discover that she will call for a definition that includes many harmful non-physical and non-sexual behaviours.[44]

At first glance, it may appear that put-downs, insults, and being publicly ridiculed do not constitute "real" abuse or cause serious harm. Rather than dismissing such behaviours as trivial, think about a teacher who picked on you or accused you unjustly of something you did not do. Do you remember a work or school situation in which you were made to feel useless, incompetent, where nothing you did could ever be right or enough, where you felt confused, did not sleep well at night, or dreaded going?[45] Many of us have gone through such incidents and probably felt angry or helpless (maybe both) as a result. Most, if not all, abused women have similar experiences, and many of them tell researchers that "they would rather be hit

---

BOX 1.5 Definition Differences Due to Disciplines

Scientists may define violence against women in ways specific to their discipline's methods of research. In addition, research questions among these different disciplines often differ, so researchers may define violence against women according to their potential uses of data. Different disciplines have different goals and objectives. Within a public health approach, measurement of violence against women may focus on factors that affect physical well-being, such as morbidity (injuries) and mortality (deaths). The focus within public health is to reduce the burden of injuries and deaths due to violence. Traditional behavioural sciences such as psychology and sociology may focus more on the risk and protective factors, consequences of being violently victimized, and treatment, because the goal is to understand human behaviour and interaction.... [C]riminologists may not use the same definitions that people employed in the criminal justice system (e.g., law enforcement, courts) use. Criminologists may focus more on the behaviour of perpetrators. Thus, measured rates can differ across and even within disciplines according to criteria selected.

Source: Desai & Saltzman, 2001, pp. 36–37.

---

than endure the constant put-downs and mind games inflicted on them by their abusive partners."[46]

Those who work with battered women know how strong many of them are and how little they worry about a few slaps and punches. Still, it is very hard for anyone to be beaten up physically and not to be simultaneously emotionally battered. As described in Chapter Five, physical battering is emotional battering. Except in the case of those women who are afraid for their lives, it is rare to hear women talk about bruises or pain. Rather, they complain about their terror of being robbed of their lives, their friends, and everything dear to them, as well as of their fear for their children. What is rarely recognized is that some men can induce such terror and psychological abuse without ever physically harming their partners. A battered women's advocate told me a few years ago about a case involving a man who beat his wife's back with a coat hanger but never hit her again. He took a picture of her bloody and bruised back and showed it to her every time he perceived her as challenging his authority. He also never said a word while showing her the picture. Needless to say, she lived in fear for her life.

People who work within the criminal justice, medical, and social service communities too often measure a woman's problems by what has been called the "stitch rule." This wry piece of humour refers to the tendency of most people to judge how badly abused a woman is by how many stitches are needed in the emergency room to close her wounds.[47] The presumption that a woman who does not need stitches was not abused is simply not the case.

More scholars, service providers, and others are now using broad definitions of violence against women in intimate relationships. Due in large part to the shortage of Canadian social-scientific research on some non-physical hurtful behaviours, this book will focus on acts of physical and sexual violence, as well as threats of such abuse. However, whenever possible, other harms are addressed, and international data will be woven into the text for comparative purposes. One form of non-lethal violence is not considered more serious than others; although a punch is often deemed to be worse than a slap, a slap can break teeth.[48] A shove can result in a fall backwards, a blow to the head, and major head trauma or death. In the next chapter, we will examine the current situation of women who experience violence in Canadian homes.

TWO

It Often Hurts to be a Woman in Canada[1]

*He's going to destroy me and he's going to ruin my
life and he told me that was his thing.*[2]

The United Nations (UN) *Human Development Report* has consistently ranked Canada as one of the best countries in terms of living standards since the early 1990s. This supports conventional wisdom, as well as the self-image of many who live here. As Jeffrey Simpson, author of the book *Star-Spangled Canadians*, correctly points out, "Canadians prefer to think of their country as virtue incarnate, its cup of tolerance running over. They endlessly recycle the cliché about Canada the 'peaceable kingdom' in large part because it makes them feel good about themselves. Canadians are peacekeepers abroad, peaceful citizens at home."[3] In addition, many outside observers regard Canada as a peaceful country.

Certainly, compared to their neighbours south of the border, Canadians are much less likely to be physically and sexually assaulted in public parks, streets, pubs, and workplaces. This is one of the key reasons why many Canadians passionately and publicly state "We don't want to be American" in response to attempts by businesses, political agencies, and other formal organizations to adopt various US policies and procedures. The mass media also contribute to Canadians' perceptions that their country is safer than the United States. On any given night, crime—especially violent acts committed by poor

African-American males—is a central feature of fictional and non-fictional US television shows.

In Canada, comparisons of political, legal, social, and economic differences between the two countries are common. Criminal justice policies and practices adopted by the federal Progressive Conservative Party under the leadership of Prime Minister Brian Mulroney from 1984 to 1990 were inconsistent with authoritarian US law-and-order models in place at that time.[4] More recently, in 2004, the Canadian government led by Liberal Party Prime Minister Paul Martin introduced a bill calling for decriminalizing marijuana possession, much to the dismay and anger of US President George W. Bush, a well-known advocate of the "war on drugs." At the start of this new millennium, Canadian law-enforcement officials were less likely to arrest and prosecute impaired drivers and sex-trade workers than were their US counterparts.

Since the mid-1990s, however, US and Canadian citizens' concerns about controlling crime and maintaining law and order have been moving closer together. In fact, some Canadian crime-control policies and laws now mirror authoritarian and gender-blind approaches advanced by US neo-conservative politicians, researchers, activists, and practitioners.[5] One key example is the omnibus Tackling Violent Crime Act, parts of which mimic failed US policies, such as the "three-strikes, you're out" sentencing law.[6] This is the result of the public's heated response to a few well-publicized murders, the ensuing media-generated moral panics, and federal politicians' attempts at election or re-election.

Although stranger-to-stranger murders are relatively rare in Canada, they are often reported for weeks and sometimes years in Canadian newspapers. On December 26, 2005, in downtown Toronto, a stranger shot and killed Jane Creba, a 15-year-old girl; three years later, her murder was still being reported in *The Toronto Star*.[7] This is not to trivialize Ms. Creba's death; it was deeply disturbing, and the pain and suffering experienced by her family and friends are immeasurable. But less sensational crimes go unreported. How often do the media report the routine sexual assaults that occur in university/college dating relationships? How frequently are male-to-female beatings in marital/cohabiting relationships featured on the evening news? And how often do the media and politicians address the plight of women killed by male ex-partners during or after the process of separation or divorce? Female victims of male violence greatly outnumber the victims of predatory violent crimes that occur on the streets and in other public places. However, the media generally characterize male-to-female assaults in intimate relationships as rare events or as the result of a man's deep-rooted psychological problems. They are not perceived as headline-grabbing incidents.

Ironically, at a time when crime discussion in Canada is dominated by calls for more prisons, reinstatement of the death penalty, and victim compensation, women who are victims of crime are often belittled. Growing numbers of conservative fathers' rights groups, academics, politicians, and others challenge research showing high rates of male-to-female beatings, sexual assaults, and other highly injurious forms of male-to-female victimization that typically occur behind closed doors and in intimate relationships. One way they do this is by arguing that women are as violent as men. This claim is erroneous and will be addressed in Chapter Three. It remains one of the greatest obstacles to improving women's health and safety, regardless of how often it is refuted by research and statistics.

The claim that women are as violent as men has been used in the United States to undermine the Violence Against Women Act (VAWA) and efforts to support it.[8] In fact, the latest version of VAWA, due in large part to the lobbying efforts of conservative men's groups, views women *and* men as victims of intimate violence and sexual assault and allows for the provision of services to men. Molly Dragiewicz reminds us that "The American Violence Against Women Act was passed in part because the existing 'gender-neutral' laws were not being enforced equitably in the context of the patriarchal subordination of women. Police failure to respond to men's violence against female intimates was pervasive prior to VAWA."[9]

Bush's attorney general John Ashcroft appointed Nancy Ptotenhauer, the former president of the Independent Women's Forum (IWF, an anti-feminist women's organization) to the Federal Advisory Council on Violence Against Women, which advises the Department of Justice and the Department of Health and Human Services on implementing the VAWA. As documented by Rhonda Hammer, the IWF was "formed in 1992 by Republican women angered by the testimony of Anita Hill at confirmation hearings for Supreme Court Justice Clarence Thomas and the prominent role played by the National Organization of Women and other feminist groups." At its meetings, Ptotenhauer frequently and publicly testified against VAWA, saying, "The Violence Against Women Act will do nothing to protect women from crime. It will, though, perpetuate false information, waste money, and urge vulnerable women to mistrust all men."[10]

Recently, the Canadian federal government took similar political action. Due in large part to the lobbying efforts of fathers' rights groups and others involved in the anti-feminist backlash, Statistics Canada now conducts surveys that no longer focus primarily on violence against women but that produce equal rates of male and female intimate violence without carefully examining their differing contexts, meanings, and motives. In addition, on October 3, 2006, Bev Oda, federal minister for the Status of Women Canada (SWC), announced that women's organizations would no longer be eligible for funding for advocacy, government lobbying, or research projects. SWC was required to delete the word *equality* from its list of goals.[11] A year later, in early September 2007, Conservative Prime Minister Stephen Harper added more fuel to an ongoing anti-feminist fire by eliminating funding to the National Association of Women and the Law (NAWL), a non-profit women's group that tackles violence against women and other forms of female victimization. It is no surprise, then, that some researchers assert that Canadians are going to see more cases where women are "twice victimized": first by violence and the men who abused them, and then by the lack of social support provided by the federal government.[12]

Shortly after the announcement about cuts to NAWL, the office of federal finance minister Jim Flaherty sent a flyer to his Whitby, Ontario, constituents' homes that included this statement: "Canada's New Government is standing up for safe communities by tackling violent crime and keeping criminals off the streets." The flyer also announced, "Serious Crime = Serious Time." Since most violence against women occurs behind closed doors and not on streets, many researchers, practitioners, and policy analysts assert that Mr. Flaherty's government does not view date or acquaintance rape, woman battering, etc. as "serious crime"—which may also explain why NAWL lost its annual funding of $300,000.[13]

The Canadian government's responses to feminist concerns are much more than a coincidence; it is clear that they are due to the ideological similarities between the former US Republican administration of George W. Bush and the current Conservative Harper government.

"UNTIL DEATH DO US PART":
INTIMATE FEMICIDE IN CANADA

Since the beginning of the war in Afghanistan in October 2001, 151 Canadian soldiers and four Canadian civilians have lost their lives there. These deaths have sparked heated debates about Canada's role in this violent conflict. An Angus Reid poll released on January 1, 2008, showed that 63 per cent of Canadians disagreed with the statement, "Canada should extend the mission in Afghanistan beyond February 2009."[14] At the same time, the federal government remained committed to continuing the war.

Politicians, journalists, and the public continue to devote considerable attention to the Afghan war. However, less notice is made of the number of women killed each year in Canada by their current or former male intimate partners. Pamela Cross, director of Advocacy and Public Policy for YWCA Canada, points out that

> It is time that the same media and political attention given
> to other victims of war be given to women killed by their
> partners. Perhaps, then, we would see that these women—who
> spend every day of their lives trying to outwit the enemy, stay
> one step ahead of him, protect the children, stay alive for
> one more day—are heroes as much as any soldier serving in
> the war.

The intimate femicide rate of 60 women per year (as well as other relevant statistics) constitutes, as Cross puts it, "a horrific and preventable death toll that should cause outrage in the citizens of this country."[15] Citizens should also be outraged by the fact that every six days in Canada a woman dies from domestic violence.[16]

The term "femicide" is two centuries old and was first used in John Corry's book *A Satirical View of London at the Commencement of the Nineteenth Century* to signify "the killing of a woman."[17] Of the various types of femicide, intimate femicide is the most common. This crime is defined as the killing of a female with whom an individual currently has, has had, or wants to have a sexual and/or emotional relationship.[18] The Ontario woman quoted at the start of this chapter was at great risk of being killed by her ex-partner in an example of yet another preventable casualty of what journalist Brian Vallée refers to as the ongoing and brutal Canadian "war on women."[19]

In Box 2.1 we see the statements "We just don't know what happened" and "We are shocked." The media's use of quotations like these makes the perpetrator's motive appear inexplicable or the result of a burst of "passion." But the truth is that this is hardly an exceptional incident. Statistics Canada researcher Valerie Pottie Bunge reports that over 75 per cent of the approximately 2,600 spousal homicides in Canada between 1974 and 2000 were of women. She further notes that homicides were decreasing since 1974, with dramatic decreases for both women (62 per cent) and men (55 per cent). She observes that

> Many recent societal changes may have contributed to the declines in spousal homicide rates including the changing nature of intimate relationships, increasing gender equality, legislative changes, policy and procedural changes such as specialized domestic violence courts, training of criminal justice personnel, and increasing availability of resources for victims.[20]

Although it is impossible to know the precise causes of homicide decreases in Canada, similar observations have been made elsewhere and have been widely attributed to the availability of services and emergency shelters for women.

BOX 2.1 Double Tragedy Turns Joy to Grief

With homicide detectives waiting outside, a team of 30 doctors and nurses fought frantically early yesterday morning to save an unborn child and her mother.

When Aysun Sesen was brought to St. Michael's Hospital with multiple stab wounds to her abdomen, her fetus still had a faint heartbeat. But when they performed a Caesarean, the girl was stillborn.

Doctors also could not save Sesen, whose husband, Turan Cocelli, 29, was charged with her slaying.

Family and friends of the 25-year-old victim congregated at an Etobicoke house last evening, some sitting despondently, others embracing, praying, and sobbing.

Instead of anticipation over Sesen's first child, expected in December, a group of relatives and members of the local Kurdish community searched for answers into this woman's death.

"We are shocked," Nirman Cocelli, a cousin, said. "We don't know what happened; we don't know what to do. Everybody is sitting around discussing it. We just try to figure out what happened."

Toronto's 64th homicide victim had been taken to hospital about 1 a.m. after emergency personnel were called to a red-brick bungalow on Whitburn Cres., near Keele St. and Sheppard Ave.

Neighbours said that while the family was quiet and kept to themselves, they could often be heard arguing.

Source: Henry & Powell, 2007, pp. A1, A10.

Research findings also document that regardless of the sex of the victim, the majority of domestic homicides are precipitated by men's violence and abuse against women and that women are at disproportionate risk following separation.

Between 1995 and 2004, domestic homicides accounted for one-third of the 4,502 solved murders in Canada. Of these, 47 per cent were spousal homicides, and four out of five involved a current or former husband against his wife. As Australian-based criminologist Kenneth Polk observes, "time and time again the phrase 'if I can't have you, no one will' echoes through the data on homicide in the context of sexual intimacy.'[21]

Note what this woman who participated in a rural Ohio study conducted from March 2003 to April 2004 went through. She still fears for her life:

> And I mean the one night he'd come home and pull a double barrel and cock both barrels and said he was going to kill me. And it was like, wait a minute here. You know, it was two o'clock in the morning. I was sound asleep and I got up at four and had to go to work. But he'd always keep pressuring me, "If you leave me, I'll find you, I'll kill you. If you leave me, I'll find you, I'll kill you."[22]

Consider these recent statistics:

- In Ontario, between 1995 and 2005, 231 women were murdered by their partners or former partners.
- Ontario's Domestic Violence Death Review Committee noted in its 2004 report that 100 per cent of the victims in the cases it reviewed were women and concluded that domestic violence is not a gender-neutral social problem. The most common risk factor was actual or pending separation, followed closely by a prior history of violence. In its 2005 report, the Committee noted that in eight out of nine cases the murder appeared predictable and preventable.
- Between 2002 and 2007, the Domestic Violence Death Review Committee noted that 94 per cent of the domestic violence homicide victims in Ontario were women.
- In 2005 in Canada, spousal homicides accounted for close to 16 per cent of all solved homicides and about half (47 per cent) of all family homicides, and women were five times more likely to be killed by their spouses.[23]

Some women are more likely to be killed than others. Separated and divorced women are at greater risk than married women. Between 1997 and 2006, women in common-law relationships accounted for the largest proportion of spousal homicide victims. During this same period, the rate of women aged 15 to 24 killed by their spouses was close to three times higher than all female victims of spousal homicide. Moreover, Aboriginal women are far more likely than non-Aboriginal women to be killed by an intimate male partner, with their rate of spousal homicide being about eight times higher.[24]

What about the risk for women belonging to other ethnic and cultural groups? At the time of writing this chapter, it is extremely difficult, if not impossible, to answer this question because of government restrictions on the collection of official homicide data (e.g., police statistics) by race or ethnicity. However, Statistics Canada is allowed to gather and report data on Aboriginal spousal murders.[25]

So, although the media tends to portray violence against women in Canada as isolated incidents, there is ample proof of ongoing systemic violence against women in this country; it is not a matter of personality disorders or other types of mental health problems. In spite of massive education efforts, many men remain unaware of the extent of male-to-female violence and how many women live in fear of their lives. Or, heavily fuelled by the anti-feminist backlash, men such as those in my undergraduate courses may respond by saying, "I don't want to hear this stuff."

MORE BAD NEWS:
SEXUAL ASSAULT IN THE LIVES OF CANADIAN WOMEN

Sexual assault is constantly on many women's minds, for valid reasons. To help sensitize university students to male–female differences about the fear of sexual assault and other types of woman abuse, I ask men in my undergraduate Violence Against Women classes to describe the techniques they use to prevent themselves from being raped. At first, none respond; eventually, one or two will say something like, "Avoid going to prison." I write this down on the blackboard under the heading "Men." Next, I ask the women to describe their avoidance strategies. A completely different picture emerges. Under the heading "Women," I write down a long list of responses, including avoiding night classes, not walking alone at night, carrying whistles and alarms, calling the campus foot patrol for escorts to the bus or a car, and a host of other preventative measures.

This exercise serves two important functions. First, it shows male students that many women worry about their safety and that their routine activities are governed by a well-founded fear of sexual assault. Second, many women who thought they were the only ones who worried about being victimized discover they are not alone or "deviant." Large- and small-scale surveys consistently show that every year approximately 25 per cent of Canadian female undergraduates experience some variation of this crime.[26] Clearly, sexual assault in intimate heterosexual relationships is normative in the statistical sense.

A burglary or robbery rate this high would turn a high school or college campus upside down; however, there is less concern when the crime involves the sexual victimization of women and girls. There are many reasons for this, but the more important are gender politics and powerful interest groups that have a stake in demonizing girls and denying the extent of sexual assaults to reassert male domination and control. In March 2006, a lawyer at a small private university in the United States stated that a recent study of unwanted sex among students at his school was flawed and revealed, at most, a high rate of "regretted sex." When asked about the possibility of victims' parents suing the university, he replied that he was more worried about lawsuits filed by "alleged perpetrators"—as if false allegations pose more of a significant problem than true ones. Note that less than two per cent of campus rapes reported to the police are false allegations.[27]

In campuses throughout North America, women are sexually assaulted "in numbers that would numb the mind of Einstein," recalling Katz's claim that "It takes a village to rape a woman."[28] Box 2.2 summarizes the experience of a woman who ran a women's centre in the same private university referred to above.

Similar situations are found in Canada. A female friend of mine was teaching at an urban Ontario university in March 2006. I will not use her name, but her experience reflects an ongoing and ever-changing pattern of misogyny among

BOX 2.2 Resistance to Making an Unsafe Learning Enviornment Safer

One woman I know runs the women's centre at a small private college in the East. In order to maintain her anonymity, I am going to paraphrase her comments. According to her, violence against women is systemically ignored and hushed up by the dean of students, who is in charge of the judicial process, policies for the student handbook, and just about every other factor that influences the kind of response that women on campus face after they have been sexually or physically assaulted. She is the person on campus with the most expertise on gender violence but is completely excluded from meetings on sexual assault and barred from providing training to the judicial board and other staff and students. She reports that in private meetings, the dean regularly yells at her, refers to rape as "regretted sex," and forbids her from talking about the concept of rape culture, which he denies exists. On her campus in 2005, a student was seriously assaulted by her ex-boyfriend in a textbook domestic violence case. Although the women's centre director provided the dean with research on the risk of escalation in cases like this and had expressed concern for the victim's ongoing safety on campus, he chose not to protect the victim. The perpetrator was back on campus the Monday following his attempt to kill his ex-girlfriend. The dean actually made the ignorant assertion that this was not a dating-violence situation, since he had asked the victim if the perpetrator had hit her before and she said no.

Source: Katz, 2006, pp. 68–69.

Canada's undergraduate student body. She received horrifying e-mail messages from male students, including some messages that threatened to rape her with a baseball bat "sooner or later." Added to some of the violent messages were pornographic pictures of women and racist statements equating people of colour with monkeys. Fearing for her life, she left her house to stay temporarily with another professor and never returned to teach her classes. A high-ranking member of the school's security department responded to her distress in a tardy, insensitive fashion until I demanded that he show up at her host's house. Shortly after he arrived, I insisted that he and a senior administrator go to her class and talk about this crime to all of the students, including a few women who were also targeted by some of the perpetrators' violent e-mail messages. My friend, a survivor of cyber sexual assault and other forms of woman abuse, will probably never return to this school, and the perpetrators were never caught. Despite all this, my friend did not react passively and did not let these atrocities drag her down. She now has an exciting career with the Ontario provincial government, but she will be dearly missed by her former university colleagues and friends.

The virtual attack described here needs to be placed in a broader social context. Both my friend's university and another institution of higher learning located near it had, up until September 2007, a ten-year history of allowing a "sex pub" to function on campus once a year. Described by its organizers as an event designed "to promote awareness" and "safe sex," the "sex pub" actually objectified women for the sake of profit and involved displays of pornographic pictures. According to one student who helped cancel this pub night, "What you're doing is commodifying sex, so in other words we can relate that to prostitution. So what are we saying to students? What are we saying about ourselves? What perception do we want to give out to students?" Further, on September 27, 2007, a woman walking to her car in the campus parking lot was repeatedly punched in the face by a male stranger, but school officials neglected to inform all the faculty, staff, and students about this attack. A few members of the campus community learned about it by reading an e-mail sent by a campus clerk to her son that included a release issued by the local police with accurate details about the beating. So much for the notion that university campuses are safe havens divorced from the hard realities of what is commonly defined as "the real world." And no arrests were made.

For the thousands of students and hundreds of teachers across Ontario and other parts of Canada, the new school year generates much excitement, hope, and optimism. It is also a time for reconnecting with old friends and for making new

TABLE 2.1 Hate-motivated sexual violence incidence rates

Type of Sexual Assault	N	Percentage
Been threatened with unwanted sexual behaviours.	14	3.7
Been sexually harassed.	8	2.1
Been verbally sexually harassed.	29	7.7
Been touched sexually when you didn't want to be touched (e.g., breasts, rear end, or genitals).	14	3.7
Had sexual relations when you didn't want to because someone threatened or used some degree of physical force (e.g., twisting your arm, holding you down) to make you.	1	.3

Source: DeKeseredy, Perry, & Schwartz, 2007.

ones. However, on Tuesday, September 2, 2008, the start of the school year turned out to be a horrific nightmare for an 18-year-old Fanshawe College student. Two men entered a common area in a student residence at this London, Ontario, school and sexually assaulted her. Although the majority of perpetrators of sexual assault are never arrested or charged, two men were charged for committing this crime. Nevertheless, many people do not seem to see these men's behaviour as symptomatic of a systemic problem.

Nothing can be further from the truth. Annually, at least one out of every four Canadian female undergraduates experiences at least one type of sexual assault. A 2006 representative sample survey of students enrolled at two Ontario post-secondary schools found that of the 384 women in the sample, slightly fewer than 11 per cent stated that they had experienced one or more of the five variants of hate-motivated sexual assault listed in Table 2.1 since their school year started.[29] As expected, the overall prevalence rate (dating from the time that the respondents were age 16) for the same items in Table 2.2 was markedly higher (27.9 per cent). This study also found a significant correlation between women who

TABLE 2.2 Hate-motivated sexual violence prevalence rates

Type of Sexual Assault	N	Percentage
Been threatened with unwanted sexual behaviours.	43	11.2
Been sexually harassed.	53	13.8
Been verbally sexually harassed.	86	22.4
Been touched sexually when you didn't want to be touched (e.g., breasts, rear end, or genitals).	59	15.4
Had sexual relations when you didn't want to because someone threatened or used some degree of physical force (e.g., twisting your arm, holding you down) to make you.	18	4.7

Source: DeKeseredy, Perry, & Schwartz, 2007.

experienced hate-motivated sexual assault and women who publicly identify themselves as feminists.[30] Thus, while the "multicultural women's movement has utterly transformed the cultural landscape" on Canadian university/college campuses, there is now evidence that on top of having to worry about abusive acts committed by male intimates and acquaintances and random acts of male "stranger danger" that "come out of the blue," many women live in fear of being attacked by their peers because of a perception that they have overstepped their boundaries. Consequently, Canadian female undergraduates must be "hyper vigilant—sometimes 24/7" about sexual assault from many different directions.[31]

Men who sexually abuse women do not suddenly turn into violent individuals upon entering university or college. On the contrary, many come to institutions of higher learning with a history of sexual aggression or a desire to engage in sexual aggression.[32] Often they were trained as far back as elementary school to treat women as sexual objects and to use women simply as things to achieve their own desire for "scoring," or engaging in sexual activity. They do not need further training when they arrive on campus. They make friends with other similarly minded men to reassure themselves that they are acting properly. Surveys conducted in Canada and the United States found that 11 to 19 per cent of adolescent boys reported having sexually assaulted girls.[33] Many young Canadian boys physically abuse girls; these boys grow up to do serious physical harm to their wives or cohabiting partners.

Additional Canadian survey data show that sexual assault is a major problem in dating, and not only in university and college relationships. Statistics Canada's 1993 Violence Against Women Survey found that 12 per cent of women had been sexually assaulted by a dating partner since the age of 16. Moreover, 16 per cent of the women aged 15 or older who participated in the 2004 GSS stated that they had been sexually assaulted by a spouse in the five years preceding the survey.[34]

Of course, not all women are at equal risk of being sexually assaulted in Canada. For example, women aged 18 to 24 are more likely to be victimized by an intimate partner or acquaintance than are older women. Reported rates of sexual assault for Aboriginal women are estimated to be four to five times higher than those for non-Aboriginal women. Other women "at the margins," including those who live in urban public housing, unemployed women, homeless women, and those who are poor, are more likely to be sexually assaulted by current or former male partners than are middle- or upper-class women.[35]

Given the lack of current in-depth research on sexual assaults on immigrant, refugee, and visible minority women in Canada, it is unclear whether members of these three groups are at higher or lower risk of being victimized than women belonging to the dominant culture. As Shahid Alvi puts it, "Compared with scholars in the United States...Canadian researchers are only now beginning to scratch the surface of the nature and extent of violence against immigrant and visible minority women."[36]

"NOBODY WANTS TO SEE": MALE-TO-FEMALE PHYSICAL VIOLENCE IN INTIMATE RELATIONSHIPS[37]

The first part of this subheading quotes the words of a rural Ohio woman interviewed for a study on separation/divorce sexual assault. She referred to the fact that in many communities—rural and urban—there is widespread acceptance of woman abuse at the same time that related norms within the community prohibit victims from publicly talking about what their husbands or male live-in partners did to them and from seeking social support. Other women told similar stories of the unwillingness of people in their community to help them. As one interviewee stated, "Nobody wants to get involved, honey." Another basically said the same thing, "No, most of 'em didn't want to get involved." Moreover, some women experienced what my former graduate student Danielle Fagen refers to as a "community backlash"[38] response to their victimization.

These women either wanted to leave, tried to leave, or have left their husbands or cohabiting partners. Canadian women have had similar experiences.[39] Like their US counterparts, when seeking legal support for themselves and their children, they are treated with disdain, as was this abused woman who participated in an Ontario study:

> So, I'm trying to deal with all of these things and I'm being thrown with the accusation that you are just doing it because you are a vindictive partner because you are trying to take his money away from him and you're doing it because.... And how come all of these things are coming all at once into the open because as soon as you left? Why is there child abuse? So why did it all of a sudden become a police case? Do you have a picture and do you have bruises and photographs and did you take them to the doctor or did you call the police?

Another woman who participated in the same study made a similar statement:

> And I feel any time I tried to talk to anyone I [was seen as] just being this vindictive ex and meanwhile I've got papers where he was charged for drinking and driving I have called CAS and I have no help.[40]

While many Canadians don't want to see or hear about what happens to thousands of women behind closed doors on a daily basis, the reality is that, annually, at least 11 per cent of women in marital/cohabiting relationships are physically abused by their male partners. Ample quantitative evidence strongly suggests that Canadian men appear to be more physically violent to adult female intimates than are their US counterparts.[41]

What is to be done about violence against women in marital/cohabiting relationships? Criminal justice officials, shelter workers, and other practitioners contend that the most important weapon women have in the battle to end their partners' abuse is to divorce or separate from them. Although many women in abusive marital or cohabiting relationships continue to live with dangerous men for reasons beyond their control such as economic dependency, most battered women eventually leave. Still, separation or divorce alone does not make them safer.

Research shows that many men refuse to leave their ex-partners alone. Their visits can be lethal, as demonstrated by statistics reviewed previously in this chapter. And there are more relevant statistics. In 16 per cent of the cases of intimate femicide that occurred in Ontario between 1974 and 1994, the victims were separated from their legal spouses. Two evolutionary psychologists found that compared to co-residing couples, separation entails a six-fold increase in homicide risk for women throughout Canada. US research also shows that separation is a key risk factor for femicide. Close to 50 per cent of the men in the United States on death row for domestic murder killed their wives or lovers in retaliation for leaving them. Approximately four women are killed by a male intimate partner every day in the United States. Statistics analyzed by the Chicago Women's Health Risk Study show that of 59 women in the homicide data set, 23 per cent were killed either just before or as they were trying to leave their partners. Indeed, data presented here and elsewhere support Diana E.H. Russell's claim that femicide is "some men's 'final solution' for women."[42]

Non-lethal separation assault is also common in Canada. Statistics Canada's national Violence Against Women Survey found that about one-fifth (19 per cent) of the women who reported violence by a previous male partner stated that the violence increased in severity at the time of separation, and 2004 Canadian GSS data show that, among women with a former husband or male cohabiting partner who had been violent during the relationship, 49 per cent were assaulted by their ex-partners after separation.[43] Several other North American studies, most of which are Canadian, uncovered similar data, with the risk of assault peaking in the first two months following separation and when women attempt permanent separation through legal or other means. It is no wonder, then, that many of Stark's female clients told him that "they were never more frightened than in the days, weeks, or months after they moved out."[44]

Like sexual assault, for many men, beatings and the like do not begin after they move in with women or marry them or after these women leave them. The CNS found the following:

- Of the 1,307 men who participated in this study, 13.7 per cent stated that they had physically assaulted their university/college dating partners in the year before the survey. Of the 1,835 female respondents, 22.3 per cent indicated that they had been physically victimized by their dating partners during the same time period.
- About 35 per cent of the women reported having been physically assaulted since leaving high school, and 17.8 per cent of the men reported having been physically abusive during the same time period.[45]

In Canada, physical violence is also common in many heterosexual adolescent dating relationships. Even at young ages, boys can develop strong sexist attitudes and beliefs. They are heavily influenced by the notion that men should be "in charge" at home and in intimate relationships. To this day, as Michael Kimmel reminds us, when asked, "What does it mean to be a man?" many male adolescents reply:

- "Boys don't cry."
- "It's better to be mad than sad."
- "Don't get mad—get even."
- "Take it like a man."

+ "He who has the most toys when he dies, wins."
+ "Just do it," or "ride or die."
+ "Size matters."
+ "I don't stop to ask for directions."
+ "Nice guys finish last."
+ "It's all good."[46]

These aphorisms come out of the mouths of boys who try to live up to the principles of what sociologist Bob Connell refers to as *hegemonic masculinity*, the dominant form of masculinity in the United States, Canada, and other countries, best exemplified by movie actors such as Tom Cruise, Brad Pitt, Clint Eastwood, Vin Diesel, and Sylvester Stallone. Unfortunately, much of North American society is devoted to convincing men and boys that they can achieve masculinity only by putting down and ridiculing everything that is female or feminine. It is not surprising, then, that 3.6 per cent of men who participated in the CNS admitted to having intentionally physically hurt one or more female dating partners when they were elementary-school students (grades 1 to 8). As expected, women reported higher rates of elementary-school dating victimization (7.2 per cent).[47]

Given that high-school students spend more time dating than those in elementary school, higher rates of disclosure were obtained from both male and female CNS participants because they spent greater time at risk for violence during their high-school years. Of the women surveyed, 89 per cent said they dated in high school, whereas 38.2 per cent said they dated in elementary school. Of the men surveyed, 87.1 per cent dated in high school and 48.3 per cent dated in elementary school. Consequently, 9.1 per cent of the women reported having been physically assaulted during a high-school date. Other Canadian studies reveal even higher rates, such as one New Brunswick study that uncovered a figure of 22 per cent.[48]

Ann Menard is one of many feminist activists and scholars who assert that physical assaults on adult women occur "in all demographic and social groups, cutting across age, race, ethnicity, sexual orientation, and economic circumstances."[49] Although her claim is factually true, male-to-female physical violence is not spread equally among these groups. An in-depth review of 14 widely read and cited studies (eight in the United States, five in Canada, and one in New Zealand) reveals major differences in violence rates obtained from married persons and cohabiters. In fact, the rate for the latter typically exceeds that of the former by two times, but the difference can be greater than four times. Cohabiting women are also more likely to experience more severe types of violence than their married counterparts.[50]

These data do not speak for themselves, and crude counts of violent behaviour must be interpreted or theorized. One interpretation offered is that marriage results in healthier relationships and is a panacea for intimate partner violence. Still, this argument is made without a careful assessment of other factors that predict violence against women, including depression, alcohol and drug abuse, living in public housing, unemployment, and men's associations with sexist or violent peers.[51]

These variables are more likely to be associated with the conditions of poverty than with marital status. Many low-income women believe that men should live up to the culturally defined role of breadwinner. The man's role as the economic provider is not only part of many women's expectations but is still fundamental to most men's self-identity. Specifically, we know that women whose male partners suffer from job instability are three times as likely to be victims of intimate violence, a situation that worsens when the couple lives in a financially disadvantaged neighbourhood. Other studies show that married men are more likely to meet the prescribed breadwinner objective than are cohabiting men and therefore are at lower risk of experiencing the gender-status inconsistency that is related to abuse. One of the fastest growing family formations has been the "wife only working" family, and research shows that this pattern is commonly tied to wife abuse. Thus, in terms of earning power, it is not only male job instability that contributes to violence but the fact that women are becoming the main wage earners in many families. Consequently, it is reasonable to speculate that although violence in marital relationships might increase because of a growing disparity in income, this trend will at least be matched in marriages created by government intrusion. This prediction is based on studies showing that "when the economic differential leans in favour of the women in the relationship, domestic violence is exacerbated."[52]

More broadly, men who feel they are unable to live up to gender expectations are more likely to abuse their partners compared with men whose ability to conform affirms their masculinity and sense of control. As more recent studies have found, the higher a woman's income, the lower the man's perception of the quality of the relationship. We also know that the rapid disappearance of male-dominated manufacturing jobs, coupled with women's increased labour-force participation and earnings, have exacerbated tensions in cohabiting relationships. This also increases the likelihood of cohabiting men's eviction from the household because their partners see them as irresponsible and/or they cannot afford to house and feed them. Thus, because married men are more likely to be employed than cohabiting men, it is not surprising that they are happier than cohabiting men because they do not face the same perceived assaults on their sense of masculinity. Further, married men are less likely to experience the same degree of emotional stress that plagues male cohabiters. This stress is a major correlate of various kinds of woman abuse found in impoverished relationships.[53]

Unemployed men drink more alcohol than those who work. Thus, it is not surprising that cohabiters have more problems with alcohol than married men. Although there is no direct cause-and-effect relationship between alcohol and woman abuse, chronic alcohol abuse is consistently found to be a strong predictor (not a direct cause) of male violence. In addition, the social context of alcohol consumption may play a stronger role than the drinking itself. For instance, a 2001 study found that Canadian university/college male students who drink two or three times a week and have male peers who support both emotional and physical violence are almost ten times as likely to assault women than are the men who do not drink or have this support.[54]

In sum, then, the reality is that cohabitation alone cannot explain why more violence occurs in cohabitation than in marriages. However, this lack of evidence does not seem to matter to those people intent on misconstruing and deliberately using crude counts of behaviour against vulnerable populations, such as poor people in cohabiting relationships.[55]

Economically disadvantaged women are also at higher risk of being physically assaulted by their male spouses. The Quality of Neighbourhood Life Survey in public housing estates in the west end of a metropolitan centre in eastern Ontario found that 19.3 per cent of the female sample reported that they had been physically assaulted by intimate partners in the year before the study.[56] This figure is markedly higher than statistics generated by national government surveys, such as the 2004 GSS.

Separated and divorced women are also at higher risk of being beaten than married women, and racial and ethnic differences are also factors. The 2004 GSS found that Aboriginal women are more than three times more likely to be victims of intimate violence than are their non-Aboriginal counterparts. The same survey also found that, between 1999 and 2004, 4 per cent of visible minority women reported having been victimized by spousal violence, while 8 per cent of other women reported experiencing such assaults. There was no difference in the rate of violence reported by recent immigrant women who arrived in Canada in 1990 and long-term immigrants (5 per cent for both groups). Nevertheless, such low figures for visible minority and immigrant women may be a function of language barriers, given that the GSS was administered only in English and French.[57] Other factors that preclude visible minority and immigrant women from revealing their violent experiences are addressed in Chapter Five.

More research demonstrating variations in male-to-female violence in intimate relationships across different socio-economic categories could easily be presented here. However, as pointed out in greater detail in Chapter Seven, a key point is that different groups of women may require different types of social support. "One size fits all" policies, albeit well intentioned, have many limitations and can be highly ineffective for many women.

WHAT SURVEY DATA DON'T TELL US ABOUT
VIOLENCE AGAINST WOMEN IN CANADA

These numbers seriously challenge the widespread belief that Canada is a non-violent country. Combined with the political and educational efforts of those struggling to end all types of woman abuse, they expose an *epidemic* of male-to-female violence in this country. However, the concept of epidemic is out of place here. To health officials, an epidemic is a disease that devastates a population before it naturally subsides. Male-to-female physical, sexual, psychological, and other forms of violence, however, seem to be deeply entrenched. Therefore, if such abuse is a disease, then it is in its *endemic* phase,[58] possibly to be compared to hard drug use (e.g., smoking crack cocaine) among truly disadvantaged North American inner-city residents. Also keep in mind that the abuse of women has existed in Western societies for centuries. Since Canadian researchers started examining this issue only in the early 1980s, we cannot conclusively state whether the rates of various types of violence against women in this country have increased or decreased over time. However, historical data suggest that today's men are no more violent, and possibly less so, than their ancestors.

Although the data presented throughout this chapter and other parts of this book tell us a great deal about the amount of violence against women, they cannot tell us about all aspects of this issue, such as the true extent of violence against women who are typically excluded from mainstream surveys. The bulk of the statistics we have noted here tend to reflect only the experiences of those people who lead relatively stable lives. If you are a student, homeowner, or a tenant who moves infrequently, you are the type of person who typically gets asked to participate in a quantitative survey. Although some surveys have attempted to include people in prisons and homeless shelters, a basic problem remains—the women abused by men are least likely to be questioned.[59]

Many homeless women, for instance, have been beaten by their male partners and forced to live on the streets because they cannot acquire adequate financial and housing support from the government or from their friends and relatives.[60]

Although they have important information to provide, they are always excluded from mainstream academic and government surveys, which rely on telephone interviewing and computer surveys rather than expensive face-to-face interview techniques. Since many women who are abused cannot afford telephones and computers, they are excluded from participating in surveys. Moreover, most quantitative procedures fail to take into account the life experiences of Canadians who do not speak English or French. The growing number of immigrant and refugee women across Canada[61] are not exempt from the types of abuse discussed here. Another group that is typically left out of statistical research are those with hearing or speech disabilities. There is no reason to assume that they are less prone to abuse. In fact, some studies show that their risk is significantly higher than that of women without disabilities.[62]

Certainly, people who are sensitive to the diverse nature of Canadian society could probably add a much longer list of people who are excluded from mainstream survey research, as well as the harms they suffer in intimate relationships (this would include psychological, economic, and spiritual abuse). However, it is beyond the scope of this book to consider all those left out of large- and small-scale Canadian surveys.

SUMMARY

Today, with so many television programs, newspaper articles, university courses, social-scientific studies, and public awareness campaigns focusing on violence against women, it is hard to imagine that less than 30 years ago this problem was largely invisible in Canada. Now, there is plenty of evidence showing that violence against women is a major social problem in this country. Yet the violent abuse of women by intimate male partners is not restricted to Western countries. It is a worldwide public health problem identified by the World Health Organization, which conducted a multi-country study of the health effects of domestic violence. Over 24,000 women who resided in urban and rural areas of ten countries were interviewed. The research team discovered that the percentage of women who had ever been physically or sexually assaulted (or both) by an intimate partner ranged from 15 to 71 per cent, with most re-search sites ranging between 29 and 62 per cent.[63]

Another major international study—the International Violence Against Women Survey (IVAWS)—interviewed 23,000 women in 11 countries. The percentage of women who revealed at least one incident of physical or sexual violence by any man since the age of 16 ranged from 1 in 5 in Hong Kong to between 50 and 60 per cent in Australia, Costa Rica, the Czech Republic, Denmark, and Mozambique. In most of the countries examined, rates of victimization were above 35 per cent. In Australia, Canada, Israel, South Africa, and the United States, 40 to 70 per cent of female homicide victims were murdered by their current or former partners. Another frightening fact is that 14 girls and women are killed each day in Mexico. Of course, male violence against female intimates takes many other shapes and forms, such as honour killings, dowry-related violence, and acid burning. Annually, nearly 5,000 girls and women are victims of honour killings around the world.[64]

Each statistical data set discussed in this book is intensely personal, a document of women's pain and suffering. Still, while many of the women who participated in the studies reviewed in this chapter have experienced harms that few people are capable of imagining, most are survivors and should not be regarded as passive victims. They are strong and brave women who have made great strides to recovery and can plan a future free of fear and pain.

THREE

"But Women Do It Too!": Understanding Women's Use of Violence in Intimate Relationships

> *He had taken my car for about a day, and I was, you know, by the time he finally returned it and everything. I was taking him home, back to his mom's house, and he tried to wreck the car. It was snowing, real bad weather, and he tried to wreck the car and everything. I got angry with him and I think I slapped him. He had said something and I said, "It is over. It is completely over." You know and he just, he just started punching me in the face and just clawing my face and punching my face and everything. And I wrestled him off and I started beating him up until he told me to stop. And then we got to his house, and then he wouldn't let me go, you know. He put his arms around me and was like trying to hold me there and everything like that. I was just crying hysterically, and his mom really didn't help too much. I mean she saw what was happening, but it was like she was frozen.*[1]

The statistics reviewed in Chapter Two, describing an unsettling truth about many Canadian women's lives, are just the tip of the iceberg. Other hurtful male-to-female behaviours in intimate relationships include psychological abuse, the destruction of prized possessions, the abuse of pets, and economic abuse. These and other forms of violence against women are not isolated incidents or the result of mental illness. Rather, they are major social problems "deeply rooted in our cultural traditions."[2] The broader social forces that motivate men to abuse women are not hidden behind closed doors and often help spawn public degradation ceremonies, such as the one described in Box 3.1.

Still, many Canadians, especially conservative men, are "stuck in gender neutral,"[3] claiming, for a number of reasons, that women are as violent as men in intimate heterosexual relationships. Martin Schwartz and I received an electronic message attacking the critique of Statistics Canada's 1999 GSS on victimization, a study that apparently shows roughly equal amounts of violence committed by men and women. The message read:

> To deny that women do not regularly, and, almost as second nature, practice the art of manipulation and control that is part of the broader definition of domestic abuse (the definition used by feminists when they conduct their research and then put it forward to promote their agenda) is simply dishonest and nefarious.[4]

Like many other similar messages I have received over the past two decades, this is extreme and vitriolic. We often hear statements such as "Women are just as violent as men." Are they really? The purpose of this chapter is to challenge the widely held notion that violence in the context of marriage/cohabitation, dating, separation/divorce, and the like is a gender-neutral problem.

THE ROLE OF THE CONFLICT TACTICS SCALE[5]

In a relatively short period of time, the social-scientific literature on gender differences in intimate partner violence has increased substantially. A growing number of scholars now theorize the complex nature of women's use of violence in intimate relationships.[6] However, as was the case roughly 18 years ago when Martin Schwartz and I responded to some researchers[7] who argued that women are just as violent as men in intimate relationships, there is still an important battle being waged over the nature of women's behaviour and its role in woman abuse. One of the key weapons used in this war is the Conflict Tactics Scale (CTS), which was developed in the 1970s by University of New Hampshire sociologist Murray Straus[8] to study violence within families. Since then the original or modified versions

---

BOX 3.1 Our First Glance in the Mirror: The Rowdy Boys

I am at the Adult Entertainment Expo in Las Vegas in January 2005. At one of the 30 exhibitor booths on the floor of the Sands Expo Center is Tiffany Holiday, a woman who performs in pornographic movies. She is kissing and touching another female performer, and a crowd of men gathers around. There are rules for how much sexual activity can take place on the convention floor, and the two women are pushing the boundary. The crowd encourages them to go further.

The other woman leaves, and Tiffany begins to simulate masturbation, all the while talking dirty to the men gathered around her. The crowd swells to about 50 men. I'm stuck in the middle, holding a microphone for a documentary film crew. Emboldened by the size of the crowd, the men's chants for more explicit sex grow louder and more boisterous. Holiday responds in kind, encouraging the men to tell her what they like. The exchange continues, intensifying to the point where the men are moving as a unit—like a mob.

Men's bodies are pressed against each other and each one vies for the best view of the woman's breasts, vagina, and anus. Many of the men are using cameras, camcorders, or cell phones to record the scene. It's difficult not to notice—not to feel—that the men pressed up against me have erections. It's difficult not to conclude that if there weren't security guards on the floor, these men would likely gang-rape Tiffany Holiday.

This is an expression of the dominant masculinity in the United States today. It is the masculinity of a mob, ready to rape.

Source: Jensen, 2007, p. 1.

---

of the CTS appear at the core of research reported in over 200 scientific journal articles and at least 30 North American books.

Although the CTS may in various studies be given only to men or only to women, the most widely cited work involves administering a survey to both partners in intact heterosexual units (married, cohabitants, dating partners). The instrument solicits information from both partners about the conflict tactics they use. It generally consists of 18 items that measure three different ways of handling interpersonal conflict in intimate relationships: reasoning, verbal aggression (referred to by some researchers as psychological abuse), and physical violence. These items are ranked on a continuum from least to most severe, with the first ten describing tactics that are not physically violent and the last eight describing violent acts. The last five items, from "kicked, etc." to "used a knife or a gun," make up the "severe violence index."

The type of "conflict tactic" used to measure violence that occurred in the past year (incidence) is generally introduced to the respondent with the following preamble. Note the ideological and factual assumptions embedded in this introduction, such as the notion that assault is the result of an "argument":

> No matter how well a couple gets along, there are times when they disagree, get annoyed with the other person, or just have spats or fights because they're in a bad mood or tired or for some other reason. They also use many different ways of trying to settle their differences. I'm going to read some things that you and your (spouse/partner) might do when you have an argument. I would like you to tell me how many times...in the past 12 months, the following has occurred....

Research suggests that the CTS is a reliable method of eliciting highly sensitive data on the least known sides of intimate heterosexual relationships. In both Canada and the United States, city-wide, provincial/state, and national representative sample CTS surveys show that at least 11 per cent of North American women in marital or cohabiting relationships are physically abused annually by their male partners. Many social scientists still consider CTS data "probably the best available when it comes to estimating the incidence and prevalence of woman abuse in the population at large."[9] Nevertheless, as has been repeatedly stated by many researchers,[10] the CTS has several key limitations and has produced data that are consistently subject to highly problematic interpretations.

Statistics Canada used a version of the CTS in its 2004 GSS and found that 7 per cent of the women and 6 per cent of the men interviewed reported at least one incident of intimate partner violence committed by a current or former spouse between 1999 and 2004.[11] These results and similar ones uncovered by other Canadian studies[12] are seized upon by some journalists, social scientists, and many fathers' rights groups to support claims that women are as violent as men and that Canada is seeing a resurgence of what Suzanne Steinmetz referred to as "the battered husband syndrome."[13] Recently, Canadian psychologist Donald Dutton claimed that "in Canada and the US, women use violence in intimate relationships to the same extent as men, for the same reasons, and with largely the same results."[14]

Do 2004 GSS data actually show that men and women are equally violent? The results are deceptive for several reasons. First, the GSS provides only raw counts of violent acts committed. As demonstrated by studies that added context, meaning, and motive measures to the CTS, a common cause of women's violence in intimate relationships is self-defence, while men typically use violence to control their partners. Some women who reported initiating violence may have sensed threats from their male partners and thus acted aggressively either to stop the overwhelming buildup of tension or because of a well-founded fear of being beaten, killed, or raped.[15]

Consider the case of Angelique Lyn Lavallee, which contributed to a landmark Canadian Supreme Court decision in 1990.[16] Lavallee was a Manitoba woman who killed Kevin Rust, the man she had been living with for almost four years. Their relationship had been volatile and punctuated by frequent arguments and abuse. In those four years, Lyn made several trips to the hospital for injuries resulting from this abuse before she finally killed him. The fatal shooting occurred on August 30, 1986, after an ongoing argument during a party at their house. Over a period of several hours, Rust hit Lavallee several times. He threatened to "get her" after the guests left. In their final encounter, he handed her a gun he had just loaded and said, "Either you kill me or I'll get you." He turned to leave, and she shot him in the back of the head.

Under the law at that time, Lavallee could expect to be charged and convicted of murder because at the exact time of the shooting she was not in grave danger of being physically attacked by Rust and therefore could not claim self-defence.

A successful claim of self-defence requires that the accused at the time of the killing had a reasonable apprehension of death or grievous bodily harm from his or her adversary and that the force used to repel this danger was necessary and reasonable. This standard is based on what an "ordinary man" would do under the circumstances.

At the first trial, the "ordinary man" standard was placed in question, and the jury acquitted Lavallee of murder. Expert evidence was given by a psychiatrist who argued that she had been terrorized to the point of feeling trapped, vulnerable, worthless, and unable to escape the relationship despite the violence. He also said that the shooting was the final desperate act of a woman who sincerely believed she would be killed that night. The jury apparently agreed with his assessment and rejected the "ordinary man" standard of the law.

However, the verdict was subsequently overturned by a majority of the Manitoba Court of Appeal, and the case was sent back for retrial. The appeal court found that the trial judge had inadequately warned the jurors of the danger of relying on the psychiatrist's opinion, which was not considered "real" evidence since much of his testimony was based on his interviews with the defendant. The case was then taken to the Supreme Court, where the judges were asked to rule on the admissibility of expert evidence and the responsibility of the trial judge in instructing the jury regarding expert testimony. The Supreme Court decision (File No. 21022), handed down in 1990, upheld the original acquittal. Since then, the use of the battered woman syndrome defence in cases involving wife-to-husband homicide has increased dramatically, but many judges in Canada and the United States still do not view abused women who fight back as being battered.[17]

Of course, some women strike some men, sometimes with the intent to injure. Still, relying on simple number counts of behaviours does not mitigate or change the conclusion that women are overwhelmingly the predominant victims of intimate adult violence. The CTS alone cannot accurately determine gender variations in intimate violence because of the following:

+ Males are more likely to underreport their violence.

- The CTS measures only conflict-instigated violence and ignores male violence use to control women or violence that may not stem from any identifiable cause (e.g., dispute, difference, or spat).
- The CTS excludes some major types of abusive male behaviour, such as forced isolation.[18]

This last point is especially important, given that Dutton and others who assert that violence in intimate heterosexual relationships is sexually symmetrical tend to obscure injurious behaviours that display marked asymmetry, such as sexual assault, strangulation, separation assault, stalking, and homicide. Rather than being an unacceptable or hysterical broadening of the definition of violence, these actions are commonly part of abused women's experiences. Nevertheless, people who assert that women are as violent as men downplay research on these forms of violence. Moreover, they pay little attention to differentiating between defensive and offensive forms of violence between intimates, a courtesy we extend to victims of other crimes.[19]

Although many of these critiques have been widely voiced for close to two decades, few researchers who use the CTS seem aware of them. However, about 14 years ago, a group of researchers, including Murray Straus, developed the CTS2 to address some of the criticisms presented in this chapter and elsewhere.[20] To meet the concern that the CTS may not elicit responses on a variety of injurious behaviours, the CTS2 includes more physical and psychological abuse items (e.g., "I called my partner fat or ugly"). To deal with the strong attack that the CTS does not measure sexual violence, the CTS2 measures seven types of sexual assault. Finally, to allow researchers to tell the difference between events that cause physical injury and those that do not (e.g., slaps that break teeth and slaps that sting but do not mark), the CTS2 includes several injury or physical outcome measures, such as "I needed to see a doctor because of a fight with my partner." All of these are positive revisions that speak directly to some of the earlier criticisms.

Still, the CTS2 does not resolve all of the problems with the original scale, especially because it continues to situate abuse only in the context of settling disputes or conflicts (the preamble remains the same). As suggested above, in effect this limitation tells the respondent to exclude reporting on abuse that is control-instigated or that does not arise from a known cause. It also does not allow the researcher to separate out aggressive abuse, whether physical or psychological, from assaults used in self-defence.

To make claims about the symmetry of violence between intimate partners, one must also conflate sex and gender. Discussions of prevalence that rely on the variables "male" and "female" cannot tell us much about gender, the socially constructed and normative set of meanings attached to these categories. This distinction is one of the primary contributions of feminist perspectives to the social sciences. Research that asks perpetrators and survivors about the nature of violence between intimates finds that both say much about gender. For example, violent men talk about threats to their masculinity when women or men fail to demonstrate adequate respect for them, whereas women talk about the normative gender expectations that abusers use to justify their violence.[21]

THE POLITICAL IMPLICATIONS OF SEXUALLY SYMMETRICAL CTS DATA

In Canada, criticisms of the CTS are dismissed by those supporters of gender-neutral definitions of violence who use terms like "family violence," "spousal violence," and "marital violence." Canadian politicians who were members of the 1998 Special Joint Committee on Child Custody and Access (SJC) publicly supported these terms. The SJC devoted considerable attention to a document submitted by fathers' rights activist Ferrel Christensen, which claimed that Canadian feminist survey researchers engage in "prostituted science and scholarship" and that violence in intimate relationships is sexually symmetrical. Obviously, Christensen and others with similar views influenced the SJC because it concluded that "because of the existence of violence against men, the Committee would not recommend that family law or divorce legislation employ a gender-specific definition of family violence."[22]

About ten years after the SJC released its report, Donald Dutton argued that "mainstream governments came to support domestic violence policy based on radical feminism."[23] This is certainly a dubious conclusion: both the 1999 and 2004 GSS focused on violence against women and men in intimate relationships, and both generated sexually symmetrical CTS data. Since it conducted its 1993 Violence Against Women Survey,[24] Statistics Canada has moved away from developing feminist surveys of violence against women and is currently being influenced by political forces guided by fathers' rights groups and others with a vested interest in minimizing the pain and suffering caused by male-to-female violence.[25] As we saw in Chapter Two, Status of Women Canada cut funding for research projects and deleted the word *equality* from its list of goals. So much for Dutton's claim that "women's rights have finally been acknowledged after centuries of religion-based political repression."[26]

MANIPULATION AND USE OF SENSATIONAL CASES

In mid-June 1998, MP Roger Gallaway, co-chair of the controversial SJC, told *Ottawa Citizen* reporter Chris Cob, "in society at large women are as equally violent as men."[27] This quotation may be more than a decade old, but the same statement is repeated today by many people from all walks of life. In addition to using problematic interpretations of CTS data to support this claim, these "backlash critics"[28] often provide anecdotal stories of sensational and statistically infrequent violent crimes committed by a few Canadian women and girls. Such an approach is not new. In fact, in 1895 Cesare Lombroso and William Ferrero detailed a number of gruesome vignettes of female murderers in *The Female Offender*, a book that continues to be influential today among conservative social circles.

Canadian journalist Patricia Pearson, author of *When She Was Bad: Violent Women and the Myth of Innocence*, is one key example of a journalist heavily influenced by Lombroso and Ferrero (see Box 3.2). To buttress her thesis about the sexual symmetry of violence, Pearson provides a detailed account of the Karla Homolka case. In the early 1990s, Homolka and

---

BOX 3.2 Lombroso's Influence in Canada

Much of what Pearson's work serves up…is old hat. Consider that Lombroso spent a good part of his book, *The Female Offender*, combing through the sensationalistic crime of violent women. Lombroso, though, spared no thought for the equity approach in violence; instead, he felt that the "female criminal is doubly exceptional, as a woman and as a criminal." Normal women, he argued, are kept on the path of virtue by "maternity, piety, weakness," which means that the "wickedness" of the female offender "must be enormous before it could triumph over so many obstacles." Lombroso then presents a series of historic and contemporary vignettes of violent women engaged in chilling and brutal crimes. His examples include mothers who killed their children, women who killed spouses and lovers, women who killed their rivals, women who killed other family members, women who instigated and enticed others to kill, and women who killed for material gain.

Now consider Pearson's chapters which include discussions of women who abuse and kill children, women who assault their spouses and lovers, and women who kill with others, and women who kill alone (including women serial killers). Pretty similar in my estimation. Also similar is the reliance on details (usually gruesome) of specific women's crimes.

Source: Chesney-Lind, 1999, p. 114.

---

her husband, Paul Bernardo, sexually assaulted and murdered three young women from Southern Ontario, one of whom was Homolka's sister.[29] These crimes, like the murder of Reena Virk described in Box 3.3, shocked and angered many Canadians and, not surprisingly, generated an unprecedented amount of media coverage. However, Pearson's account of the Homolka case does not prove that women are equally as violent as men, and it is not a typical example of female violence. Throughout North America, females account for only 12 per cent of all serial killers.[30] Furthermore, no reliable study has found that men

---

BOX 3.3 The Murder of Reena Virk

On 14 November 1997, 14-year-old Reena Virk, a girl of South Asian
origin, was brutally murdered in a suburb of Victoria, British
Columbia. Reena was first beaten by a group of seven girls and
one boy, all aged between 14 and 17. She was accused of stealing
one of the girls' boyfriends and spreading rumours. Her beating
was framed as retaliation against these alleged actions. According
to journalistic accounts, the attack began when one of the girls
stubbed out a cigarette on her forehead. As Reena tried to flee, the
group swarmed her, kicked her in the head and body numerous
times, attempted to set her hair on fire, and brutalized her to the
point where she was severely injured and bruised. During the beating, Reena reportedly cried out, "I'm sorry" (Hall, 1999, p. A10).

  Battered, Reena staggered across a bridge, trying to flee her
abusers, but was followed by two of them—Warren Glowatski
and Kelly Ellard. The two then continued to beat her, smashing
her head against a tree and kicking her to the point where she
became unconscious. They then allegedly dragged her body into
the water and forcibly drowned her. Reena's body was found
eight days later, on 22 November 1997, with very little clothing on
it. The pathologist who conducted the autopsy noted that Virk
had been kicked 18 times in the head and her internal injuries
were so severe that tissue was crushed between the abdomen
and backbone. She also noted that the injuries were similar to
those that would result from a car being driven over a body. The
pathologist concluded that Reena would probably have died even
if she had not been drowned.

Source: Jiwani, 2006, p. 68.

---

and women are equally likely to sexually abuse members of the
opposite sex.

  Contrary to what the media may say, Homolka and the
girls who harmed Reena Virk are not typical Canadian female
offenders. Nor do we see a major surge in female youth violence
such as that described in James Garbarino's recent controversial book *See Jane Hit*.[31] Nevertheless, such characterizations of
violent women persist in such popular movies as *Single White*

Female, Basic Instinct, Fatal Attraction, The Hunger, and *The Hand that Rocks the Cradle. Monster,* a 2003 movie, was based loosely on the life of female serial killer Aileen Wuornos, who killed seven men in the late 1980s and early 1990s. Charlize Theron won the Academy Award for Best Actress for her portrayal of Wuornos as a masculine premeditating murderer.

> The film used several strategies to masculinize the character of Lee Wuornos. She is dressed in men's clothing, she is depicted as physically larger and dominates her petite, more feminine partner...Christina Ricci, who in no way physically resembles [Wuornos's] real-life partner, Tyria Moore. Wuornos is depicted as the sole provider and the one who controls physical contact in the relationship. Placing the film's killing spree entirely within a nine-month time frame beginning with the initiation of her intimate relationship with a woman implies that her lesbian relationship, rather than her appalling life circumstances up to that point in her life, were to blame for her murders. Even the title suggests that to be lesbian and to be violent casts one into a non-human role. For a movie that is supposed to be sympathetic to the horribly abused Wuornos, to name the film *Monster* is to perpetuate myths about the woman.[32]

Books and movies about sensational cases of female violence, combined with anti-feminist rhetoric, have contributed to a moral panic about women's use of violence at home and elsewhere.[33] The concept of moral panic was developed by Stanley Cohen to describe a situation in which a condition, episode, person, or a group of persons come to be defined as a threat to society. The media, together with some social scientists, lawyers, agents of social control, and other "experts," have jumped on the bandwagon to transform girls and women who violate a myriad of patriarchal gender norms in the United States, Canada, and other parts of the world into folk devils: "a socially constructed, stereotypical carrier of significant social harm." Such women are labelled as being made up of "sugar and spice and everything evil."[34]

Moral panics about girls have been around for decades, but they are, as Mike Males puts it, now "setting records for ferocity."

He offers rich evidence of the selective inattention given to the harsh realities many girls face today. What is especially disturbing, he observes, is that on top of trivializing violence and other harms inflicted on girls, some journalists, academics, and others profit politically, socially, and economically from belittling or demonizing their many legitimate achievements.[35] Although many young women around the world today face hardship and live in fear of violence, Males presents reputable survey data showing that most girls in contemporary North America are happy, having fun, and not on the path to becoming "unruly women."[36]

Listening to girls' voices is deemed radical by most North Americans and the politicians who represent them because Canadian and US laws still view children as powerless and the personal property of their parents. However, progressive child activists and highly respected scholars around the world, including those who do not identify themselves as feminists, agree with Males's arguments. Moreover, child participation in the creation and implementation of policies and laws that affect them is a key ingredient of the UN Convention on the Rights of the Child (UNCRC), which was adopted by the UN General Assembly in 1989 and came into effect September 2, 1990. Approximately 191 countries have ratified the UNCRC, but Somalia and the United States want no part of it.[37]

There are several causes for this reluctance to listen to adolescents. Elliott Currie's interviews with troubled middle-class boys and girls sensitize us to the role of modern social Darwinist culture. Problems often start in families, "which often embody the 'sink or swim' ethos of the larger culture—a neglectful and punitive individualism that sets adolescents up for feelings of failure, worthlessness, and heedlessness that can erode their capacity to care about themselves and others." Currie found that "there is no help out there" for many delinquent youth raised in households that encourage "the survival of the fittest."[38] In fact, teachers and therapists who use techniques influenced by Darwinian thought exacerbated his interviewees' problems.

In Canada and the United States where the politics of division and media-induced moral panics too often overrule logic, money tends to flow to the issues du jour, rather than to the most important problems. Barry Glassner asks whether we are afraid of the wrong things: terrorist attacks, road rage, methamphetamine addiction, rape drugs, school shootings, "girls gone wild," and other rare events that are too often exploited by the media that most people follow. Meanwhile, statistically frequent problems are ignored: homelessness; the lack of proper medical care, particularly for children and pregnant women (leading to a truly embarrassingly large infant mortality rate); malnourishment of children; extraordinarily low literacy rates; and the alarming number of girls who are beaten, raped, and abused in many ways. Moreover, while many people, especially men, are quick to point out human rights violations in totalitarian countries, they simultaneously whitewash or ignore the victimization of women in their own so-called democratic societies.[39]

TYPOLOGIES OF INTIMATE PARTNER VIOLENCE AND ABUSE[40]

Some scholars, such as Michael Johnson,[41] attempt to bridge or explain the gap between gendered and gender-neutral theories of violence by offering typologies. It may be useful to observe that the type of violence labelled as coercive control, woman abuse, battering, or intimate terrorism is qualitatively different than infrequent, non-injurious acts that invoke no fear or coercion. However, studies based on the CTS or other de-contextualized measures provide no information that can be used to characterize incidents as representative of one type of violence or another. Furthermore, as we have seen above, it is impossible to make accurate claims about the motives of violence based on the number of acts committed within a given time. Certainly, motivations for violent and controlling behaviour vary, and even Johnson readily admits that "qualitative research and rich interview data would be necessary to thoroughly understand the meaning and social context [of intimate partner violence]."[42]

Another problem with Johnson's typology is that he claims to identify a very small number of cases that to him exemplify "mutual coercive control," in which

[b]oth members of the couple are violent and controlling,
each behaving in a manner that would identify him or her as
an intimate terrorist if it weren't for the fact that their partner
also seems to be engaged in the same sort of violent attempt to
control the relationship.[43]

What makes this assertion highly problematic is that, as Evan
Stark puts it, while there is evidence that *some* women often
use force to control their male partners, "they typically lack the
social facility to impose comprehensive levels of deprivation,
exploitation, and dominance found in coercive control. I have
never encountered a case of coercive control with a female
perpetrator and male victim."[44]

As of yet, typologies such as Johnson's are speculative and
their application is therefore premature. Moreover, some critics caution that typologies are likely to be misused. Pence and
Dasgupta, for instance, note that it is all too easy for abusers
and their allies to paint individual incidents as "situational" or
aberrant even when they are not, and that this can have life-
and-death consequences. Although shelter staff and scholars
recognize that not all violence is the same, and not all violence
that takes place in the home is necessarily battering, there is
no tool that can discern whether an individual act is part of a
broader pattern of coercive control. Accordingly, anti-violence
advocates continue to call for assessments that place violence
and abuse in the context of the relationship, family, community,
culture, and history.[45]

SUMMARY

According to Donald Dutton, the statement that "women are
never violent except in self-defence" is one of the "bedrock beliefs in feminist theory."[46] This is inaccurate. Feminist scholars
have been at the forefront of research on women's and girls'
use of violence. The journal *Violence Against Women* published
a three-part special issue titled "Women's Use of Violence in
Intimate Relationships" in 2002 and 2003 (Volume 8, Numbers
11 and 12; Volume 9, Number 1). The same widely read and
cited journal published another issue titled "Intimate Partner

Violence: Debates and Future Directions" (Volume 12, Number 13) that also focused on women's use of violence. Undoubtedly, many feminist and non-feminist scholars are deeply committed to enhancing a rich empirical and theoretical understanding of women's use of violence. Nevertheless, as stated before, while *some* women hit men without provocation, the bulk of violence in intimate heterosexual relationships is committed by men.

Unfortunately, an enormous audience exists for what Schwartz and DeKeseredy refer to as "people without data," whose claims that women are as violent as men are constantly disseminated through the media.[47] These views have the potential to cause woman abuse survivors considerable pain and suffering, and they can give government officials an excuse to deny abused women social support services, such as shelters. It is important to remind people, including journalists and politicians, of the following information in addition to other data that challenge the erroneous claim that violence in marriage, dating, and the like is sexually symmetrical:

+ Ninety to 95 per cent of the requests for police assistance in domestic violence are from or on behalf of women.
+ Women are much more likely to be injured than are men in disputes or conflicts involving violence.
+ Even when both men and women are injured, women's injuries are about three times as severe as men's injuries.
+ Hospital data show women to be overwhelmingly the injured parties in domestic assaults.
+ There is no evidence that many men seek emergency and/or safe accommodation, such as in shelters for battered women.[48]

We shall now turn in Chapter Four to an examination of who commits violence in Canada and why.

FOUR

"Who Would Do Such a Thing?": Explaining Violence Against Women in Canada

One of the obstacles to recognizing chronic mistreatment in relationships is that most abusive men simply don't seem like abusers. They have many good qualities, including times of kindness, warmth, and humour, especially in the early period of a relationship. An abuser's friends may think the world of him. He may have a successful work life and have no problem with drugs or alcohol. He may simply not fit anyone's image of a cruel or intimidating person. So when a woman feels her relationship is spinning out of control, it is unlikely to occur to her that her partner is an abuser.[1]

Why do men assault the women they love or are sexually involved with? The most common answer is that they must be "sick" or mentally ill. How could a "normal" person punch, kick, stab, rape, or shoot someone he deeply loves and depends on? Certainly, the media help to build that myth: violence against female intimates is generally portrayed in novels, television, and films as involving a drunken, pathological, foreign, or criminal assailant.[2]

Even for me—a sociologist—it is difficult sometimes to see men who assault or kill women as anything other than sick. Consider what happened to this person I interviewed in rural Ohio in 2004. Janet was one of several women who was forced to have group sex and then beaten after going through brutal degradation ceremonies:

He ended up bringing someone into the relationship, which I
didn't want, but he told me that if I didn't do it he would leave
me. And I ended up staying with him. He was more into group
sex and, uh, trying to be the big man. He wanted sex in a group
thing or with his buddies or made me have sex with a friend
of his. See one time he made me have sex with a friend of his
for him to watch, and then he got mad and hit me afterwards.
I mean he tied me up so I could watch him have sex with a
13-year-old girl. And then he ended up going to prison for it.
So, I mean it was nasty.[3]

The many men, like Janet's husband, who abuse their
intimate female partners are not sick (see data in Chapter
Two). Although such violence is occasionally a function of
psychopathology, most abusive men are "less pathological than
expected," with only 10 per cent of all incidents of intimate violence resulting from mental disorders.[4]

THE LIMITATIONS OF PSYCHOLOGICAL EXPLANATIONS

Psychological explanations for violence against women may be
common, but they are not as popular among social scientists as
they were in the 1970s. Nevertheless, several prominent researchers, such as Donald Dutton, whose work I've cited before, still
claim that the majority of men who beat, kill, or sexually assault
their current or estranged female intimate partners do so because they are mentally ill or suffer from personality disorders.
Much of the popular British sensibility on battered women was
formed on the parallel theory, popularized by J.J. Gayford, that
the women themselves can be seen as deviant or mentally ill,
thus bringing violence upon themselves. Even today, there is a
propensity for many male psychiatrists to blame female victims
for their male partners' abusive behaviour.[5]

There are some worrisome aspects to these explanations.
If violent husbands, cohabiting and ex-partners, and boyfriends
are in fact mentally ill, then why do they only beat their current or former female partners and not their bosses, friends, or
neighbours? Admittedly, many men do attack these others, but
men who beat women in intimate relationships generally do

not have convictions for violence outside the home. If these men have terrible problems with self-control, how do they manage to keep from hitting people until they are home alone with their loved ones? If they are "out of control," then why do they only beat their partners instead of killing them? These questions cannot be answered by psychological theories, which largely ignore the unequal distribution of power between men and women in North American society and in domestic contexts.[6]

Although policy proposals will be addressed later in this book (see Chapter Seven), it is worth mentioning here that one tends to locate the solution in the same place where one locates the problem. Thus, if the problem of male-to-female violence is one of the mental health of men, then the solution is to treat, "fix," or punish the men so that they will behave according to the dominant social order.[7] However, many men are motivated to victimize women by their peers and by other social pressures. Policies that attack only the individual do nothing to address these factors. Dealing with one man at a time will never solve the broader problem. For instance, many violent men are also substance abusers. Curing their addiction will not cure their violence because most abusive men continue to physically, sexually, and psychologically harm female intimates even after they have reached sobriety. Contrary to popular belief, "[t]here is no conclusive empirical evidence to support a causal relationship between abuse and alcohol or other drug use or abuse."[8]

Sociological criticisms of psychological theories are not well received by either the general public or many policy-makers, especially in the United States, partly because that country is "the world capital of psychological-mindedness and therapeutic endeavour."[9] Approximately one-half of the world's clinical psychologists and one-third of the world's registered psychiatrists work in the United States. New York City alone has more psychoanalysts than any European country, to say nothing of the enormous number of psychiatric social workers, holistic healers, therapists of dozens of schools of thought, and others who can afford an office and a couch.[10] Although to a lesser extent, Canada, too, is a therapeutic society that supports an array of self-help books and therapists, and criminal behaviour is typically seen as a property of the individual. There are over 200 psychological programs for violent men in Canada, another example of "psychologizing and decriminalizing" violence against women.[11]

EXPLAINING VIOLENCE AGAINST WOMEN:
THE NEED FOR A SOCIOLOGICAL IMAGINATION

If only a handful of Canadian men hit, beat, raped, and killed women, it would be easy to accept non-sociological accounts of their behaviour: they must be disturbed individuals. Unfortunately, male-to-female violence in intimate relationships is deeply entrenched in our society.[12] Therefore, sociologists ask, given the widespread nature of domestic crimes in Canada, how can we maintain that they are committed only and always by pathological individuals? To demonstrate this would require intensive study to prove whether Canadian society has more "sick" individuals than other countries. We cannot completely reject individualistic explanations, which do help make sense of criminal acts committed by *some* people. Clearly, there are those whose biological or psychological problems are factors in their decision to assault women and who have been stopped from committing future crimes through the use of therapy, psychotropic drugs, and other psychologically and biologically informed treatments.[13]

We need to develop a *sociological imagination*, as Mills titled his 1959 treatise, to best explain violence against women in Canada. This perspective calls for an understanding of how *personal troubles* are related to *public issues*. Personal troubles are just what you might think. If you are raped, robbed, beaten, or cheated, you have a problem and you have to deal with it. You may need medical attention, comfort from friends or family, financial help, or some other form of aid. Sometimes, however, many people are suffering individually from the same personal problem at the same time. If ten women are raped in one year on a university campus, each one of these women has a personal problem. At the same time, broader structural and cultural forces—such as patriarchy or capitalism, Mills would argue—allows for many women to be victimized. To look beyond the personal troubles of one or two female students who have been sexually assaulted and see the broader problem of rape on campus and its causes is to possess the sociological imagination.

At first glance, we might assume that a man who assaults the woman with whom he shares an intimate relationship must either be suffering from stress or be mentally ill. That may seem an adequate explanation for the two or three cases that we know personally. However, when we look at the ii per cent or so of women in Canadian marital/cohabiting relationships who are physically abused annually by their male partners, we find "an indication of a structural issue having to do with the institutions of marriage and the family and other institutions that bear upon them."[14]

With this rationale for analyzing violence against women, we will now examine some key sociological factors that contribute to rapes, beatings, femicide, and the like. It is impossible to simply pick out one "reason" and announce that it covers all cases at all times. Indeed, violence against women is multidimensional in nature: women in a broad variety of situations are assaulted in a broad variety of ways by a broad variety of men. As Elizabeth Stanko observes, "For the most part, women find that they must constantly negotiate their safety with men—those with whom they live, work, and socialize, as well as those they have never met."[15]

PORNOGRAPHY

At London, Ontario's Fanshawe College, on September 26, 2008, University of Western Ontario scholar Dr. Helene Berman gave a powerful presentation at a conference titled "Overcoming Violence in the Lives of Girls and Young Women: Stories of Strength and Resilience." She asked the audience to imagine what an anthropologist from outer space would see if she or he came to study Canadian society. As well as the beautiful landscape, people involved in scholarly and athletic activities, and many other positive things, the anthropologist would be hard pressed not to notice an alarming amount of pornographic images on television, in magazines, in video outlets, and elsewhere, many of them including children (see Box 4.1). Translated from the Greek, the word "pornography" means "writing about prostitutes." Following Diana E.H. Russell, we will define pornography here as "material that combines sex and/or exposure of genitals with abuse or degradation in a manner that appears to condone or encourage such behaviour."[16]

As Ontario Provincial Police Chief Julian Fantino said in the interview cited in Box 4.1, "There's money to be made here" and "The Internet knows no boundaries." In the United States, annual revenues from various pornography outlets come to US$15 billion, and it is estimated that more than 28,000 Internet users pay to view pornography every second. This is more money than comes from the sales of tickets for baseball games, movies, and music concerts combined. According to the Internet Filter Review, worldwide pornography revenues, including in-room movies at hotels, sex clubs, and Internet sex sites, topped $97 billion in 2006—more than the combined revenues of Microsoft, Google, Amazon, eBay, Yahoo!, Netflix, and Earthlink.[17]

Increasingly pornography is becoming more "normalized" or "mainstreamed," despite being more violent and racist. In fact, as Robert Jensen, author of the widely read and cited book *Getting Off: Pornography and the End of Masculinity*, told *London Free Press* journalist Ian Gillespie, "It's become almost as common as comic books were for you and me."[18] Anyone who has a satellite dish or cable television has easy access to pornography channels, many of which are viewed by Canadian youth.

To make matters worse, what young people are watching is not harmless or simply "dirty pictures that have little impact on anyone." Rather, the images typically portray "women as second-class citizens" and "requires that women be seen as second-class citizens."[19] This is what Robert Jensen viewed during his analysis of a bestselling pornography video:

> One of the ten scenes in the film *Gag Factor #10*, a 2002 release
> from J.M. Productions, begins with a woman and a man
> having a picnic in a park. He jokes about wanting to use the
> romantic moment to make love to her mouth, and then stands

BOX 4.1 Huge Porn Bust Frees Two Children

Searing images of the sexual abuse of infants, toddlers, and schoolchildren from across Ontario make up the evidence in the largest child pornography bust in Ontario history, police say.

The cross-Ontario raids freed a 4-year-old Ottawa boy and 12-year-old Burlington girl this week, but police said they fear there are plenty of other children still suffering from sexual abuse and exploitation on the Internet.

"For those children waiting to be rescued, we are looking for you," Inspector Andrew Steward of the Ontario Provincial Police said. "Tell someone."

His comments came yesterday at a news conference as officers from 18 Ontario forces announced the arrests of 31 men and boys charged with child pornography and sexual abuse and exploitation on the Internet....

"The most fundamental responsibility of our society is to protect our children," Ontario Provincial Police Commissioner Julian Fantino said.

"Such cases include images of penetrative sexual activity between adults and very young children and infants, sexual bondage of children, bestiality and increasingly 'live' web-cam streaming of real-time abuse of infants and children," according to information released by police at the news conference....

Some of the people trafficking porn images are child molesters, while others are organized criminals, police said.

"There's money to be made here," Fantino said.

But police said studies show 19 of 20 cases of child sexual abuse in Canada likely go undetected.

Fantino used the news conference to push for a Cross-Canada sexual abuse registry.

"The Internet knows no boundaries," he said.

Source: Edwards, 2009, p. A3.

---

and thrusts into her mouth while she sits on the blanket. Two other men who walk by join in. Saying things, such as "Pump that face, pump that fucking face," "All the way down, choke, choke...." One man grabs her hair and pulls her head into his penis in what his friend calls "the jackhammer." At this point she is grimacing and seems in pain.[20]

This is not an extreme example; hurtful pornography has become normalized. As Jensen notes:

> There is no paradox in the steady mainstreaming of an intensely cruel pornography. This is a culture with a well-developed legal regime that generally protects individuals' rights and freedoms, and yet it also is a strikingly cruel culture in the way it accepts brutality and inequality. The pornographers are not a deviation from the norm. Their presence in the mainstream shouldn't be surprising because they represent mainstream values: the logic of domination and subordination that is central to patriarchy, hyper-erotic nationalism, white supremacy, and a predatory corporate capitalism.[21]

More evidence of the normalization of violent pornography is provided in Box 4.2 The computer "game" described there would still be sold online by Amazon.com if it were not for angry protests by some British politicians and game buyers.

Canadian and US research consistently shows that pornography is strongly associated with various types of violence against women. The CNS found that of the 1,268 female respondents who had dated during their post-secondary careers, 8.4 per cent stated that they were upset by dating partners and/or boyfriends trying to get them to repeat acts seen in pornographic pictures, movies, or books. Of the women who were forced into sexual acts since leaving high school, 23 per cent had also been upset by attempts to get them to imitate pornographic scenarios. Only 5.8 per cent of the women who were not sexually victimized reported being upset by pornography.[22]

South of the border in rural Ohio, of the 43 women I interviewed who were sexually assaulted during or after the process of separation/divorce, 30 per cent stated that pornography contributed to sexually abusive events.[23] Many other studies conducted across North America support the finding that pornography often serves as a training manual for assault.[24] But does pornography directly cause violence against women? On

> **Box 4.2 Amazon Declines to Sell "RapeLay" Video Game**
>
> Withdrawn from sale: Amazon.com has stopped selling RapeLay, in which players have to stalk and rape a family of women.
>
> In RapeLay, gamers direct a character to sexually assault a mother and her two young daughters at an underground station, before raping any of a selection of female characters.
>
> The game was intended for release just in Japan, but was on offer to British buyers through Amazon Marketplace, the section of the online store's website to third-party sellers.
>
> But Amazon has now withdrawn the game after complaints from users, deeming it to be inappropriate. "We determined that we did not want to be selling this particular item," a spokeswoman said.
>
> RapeLay was developed by the Japanese production house Illusion, which makes a number of sexually violent games for the domestic market. Their other titles include "Battle Raper" and "Artificial Girl."
>
> A spokesman for the company said: "We believe there is no problem with the software, which has cleared the domestic ratings of an ethics watchdog body."
>
> Keith Vaz, the Labour MP for Leicester East who has previously spoken out against computer games that promote violence, condemned the game.
>
> Source: Kome, 2009, p. 1.

the one hand, it may well be that for men who physically and sexually abuse women, pornography is just one more weapon in their arsenal. A man who knows that his partner would be scared or angry might not try to expose her to the lessons he learned from a pornographic movie, while his abusive friend might try to force his female partner to act out such scenes over her objections. In a somewhat related argument, it might very well be that the same factors that cause a man to abuse women also cause him to view and purchase pornography. In other words, the abuse comes first, followed by an interest in pornography. In these scenarios, eliminating pornography might not have an effect on the amount of woman abuse, since the men are generally abusive anyway.

On the other hand, since an unknown number of men who consume pornography never abuse women, the assertion that porn is a key determinant of male-to-female violence can be refuted. However, as Russell notes:

> This is comparable to arguing that because some cigarette smokers don't die of lung disease, there cannot be a causal relationship between smoking and lung cancer. Only members of the tobacco industry and some seriously addicted smokers consider this a valid argument today.[25]

Reputable studies show that many women have been harmed or were upset by their partners' requests or demands to imitate pornographic scenarios. Moreover, close to 60 years of North American research reveals that *male peer support* is a powerful determinant of various types of male-to-female abuse.[26]

MALE PEER SUPPORT

A few studies have found that the contribution of pornography to violence against women is related to male peer support.[27] Some men learn to sexually objectify women through their exposure to pornographic media, and they often learn these lessons in groups, such as at pornographic film showings at fraternity houses.[28] Some of the fraternity brothers interviewed by anthropologist Peggy Reeves Sanday stated that

> [S]eeing pornography is something to do before their parties start. They want to learn what it's like to "have a two-foot dick" and to have a good time together. They never go alone, always together. They go together in order to have a good time, laugh, and make jokes during the movie. They disassociate themselves from the men who go alone to porno movies downtown and sit in seats "with coats and newspapers spread out over their laps" and "jerk off" during the movie. They believe this is sick, but they don't think "getting off" while reading

68

Playboy privately or enacting a porno fantasy in their house is necessarily sick.[29]

Similarly, some rural Ohio survivors of separation/divorce sexual assault said that their partners consumed pornography with their male friends while drinking excessive amounts of alcohol. Agnes is one woman who experienced this problem:

> They were drinking and carrying on and they had, um, they had a bunch of porno stuff in the garage and I had walked in and I had started to tear it up. And I was, I was, I thought it was gross. I was mad at it. I was mad at him for being around it. And he just started charging after me and I started running to my car as fast as I could. And he got into the car and he threw me down in the seat and he just kept punching me, punching me.[30]

Peer culture occupies an equally important position in Canada, where, like youths who engage in violent street gang activities, many wife beaters, date rapists, stalkers, and so on are what criminologist Mark Warr refers to as "companions in crime."[31] In other words, they are heavily influenced to engage in woman abuse by male peer support. There are a variety of sociological and social psychological processes by which patriarchal and/or violent peers influence men to abuse women, but the key point is that such all-male groups encourage, justify, and support the abuse of women by their members. They provide informational support, guidance, and advice that influence men to sexually abuse their partners. Male peer-support theories developed and tested by Martin Schwartz and me see such support as a motivational factor, allowing men to develop pro-abuse attitudes and behaviours as a result of the encouragement and support of other males, if not the broader culture at large.

As US criminologist Lee Bowker[32] discovered nearly 28 years ago, male peer support for the development of a sexist subculture of violence is not restricted to one specific time, place, or socio-demographic group. There is much recent evidence supporting his claim. The CNS found a relationship between sexual abuse and two key variants of male peer support: (1) attachments to male peers who physically, sexually, and psychologically abuse their dating partners; and (2) friends who verbally encourage the physical, sexual, and psychological abuse of dates or girlfriends in certain situations, such as challenges to patriarchal authority. Similarly, a study of Canadian public housing shows that sexist male peer support promotes wife beating, sexual assault, and other injurious patriarchal practices.[33]

Male peer pressure that legitimates the sexual objectification of women and the sexual and/or physical abuse of them is also found among inner-city African-American men in Chicago, among poor African-American boys in parts of St. Louis, in rural Ohio and Kentucky, and in rural New Zealand and rural South Africa.[34] There is also evidence of the emergence of pro-abuse male peer-support groups in cyberspace. Although the precise number is unknown, exploratory research shows that many men, most of whom probably have never had face-to-face contact with each other, share violent pornographic material through e-mail and other electronic channels. These are not innocent users who accidentally come across images, voices, and texts. Nor are they constantly bombarded with such material. Rather, they choose to consume and distribute "cyber porn"; some of them commit criminal acts in the process.[35]

Patriarchal male peer support also contributes to the perception of damaged masculinity among many men during and after separation/divorce and motivates them to physically and sexually "lash out against the women...they can no longer control."[36] If a patriarchal man's peers see him as a failure with women because his partner wants to leave or has left him, he is likely to be ridiculed because he "can't control his woman." In the eyes of his peers, he has not lived up to their high expectations for male-appropriate behaviour and, therefore, must be held accountable. Hence, in the same way that university men rape women to confirm their masculinity, he is likely to sexually assault his partner to regain status among his peers. Similar to other men who rape female strangers, acquaintances, or dates, the sexual assaults committed by men during or after the process of separation/divorce may have much more to do with their need to sustain their status among their peers than to satisfy their sexual desires or a longing to regain a loving relationship.[37]

Mark is a young man who describes how the intense male peer pressure to have sex "eclipses pleasure":

> I remember there was this party, and all my buds are telling me that there is this really hot girl who sorta likes me, and, like, I already had a girlfriend back home, but they were like all, "Who cares, dude? It's a party and she's hot!" and so I got a little drunk, got her a little more drunk, and we had sex and like the whole time it was because I had to tell the guys I did her, you know? I didn't even really like her or anything. But they would have been on my case forever if I passed it up. I think I had sex not because I wanted to have sex, but because I wanted to have *had* sex—so I could talk about it. How fucked up is that?[38]

A MALE-DOMINATED SOCIETY

Contrary to what some evolutionary scholars assert,[39] over time men have not been biologically programmed or "hardwired" to sexually and/or physically abuse women. If this were true, then all men would be violent toward women, but most are not. Those who are choose to act violently and choose to associate with men who encourage and support such actions.[40] However, violent male behaviour toward women and male peer-support dynamics do not operate in a vacuum. Men learn a substantial number of actions, values, and beliefs from growing up in and being part of the larger North American culture. Their values and beliefs are micro-social expressions of broader social forces, which in Canada and the United States are too often patriarchal forces.[41]

What does it mean to say that our society is marked by patriarchy? Not surprisingly, defining patriarchy is the subject of much debate. For simplicity, let us say that patriarchy is "a sexual system of power in which the male possesses superior power and economic privilege."[42] As we saw in Chapter Two, there is ample evidence that men in general have more power and privileges than do women in Canada. Amazingly, though, there are a number of anti-feminist scholars and conservative men's groups who argue to a receptive audience that the reverse is true: that women often have the upper hand and that feminist politics are becoming deeply entrenched in the labour market, provincial and federal governments, and other institutions. Unfortunately, in Canada,

+ Women make up only 5 per cent of skilled trades, 10 per cent of fire and police departments, and 26.3 per cent of senior managers.
+ Women make up only 22 per cent of professionals in the natural sciences, engineering, and mathematics.
+ Thirty-five per cent of women have not completed high school, and 72 per cent of these women had median after-tax incomes under $13,786.
+ Women are underrepresented by almost a three-fold factor in the top 20 per cent of Canadian wage earners. Only 11 per cent get to the top 20 per cent, while 29 per cent of men access these incomes of $32,367 and above.
+ Women aged 45 to 64 made only 51 per cent of the wages of their male counterparts.[43]

There are many more statistics that reveal glaring examples of gender inequality. Still, Canadians, like US citizens, keep hearing that the women's fight for equality "has largely been won."[44] Why, then, is the female poverty rate so high compared to men, and why are at least 11 per cent of Canadian wives/cohabiting partners beaten by their male partners at least once each year? The answer is that many Canadians, especially conservative affluent males, benefit from these and other forms of gender inequality. They have no interest in eliminating patriarchy and in fact are determined to strengthen it.

Nevertheless, Canadian feminists and other progressives periodically find reasons to be optimistic. Although Canada is a patriarchal country, every major social institution, such as the family, the workplace, and the military, has been affected by equality laws and other means of eliminating sexism.[45] Still, as Stanko reminds us, "Despite the advantages for some women who have achieved educational and employment recognition, our concern about physical and sexual integrity remains one of our main worries"; moreover, "there is little evidence that the general patterns of men's abuse have been interrupted."[46]

Violence against women is a type of communicative work, and the harm it causes is both physical and symbolic. Such behaviour is also gendered and is a means of coercive control used to maintain male power and domination. A Toronto survey of wife beating found that men who espouse the ideology of *familial patriarchy* are more likely to beat their wives than men who do not. Similarly, the CNS found that male undergraduates who physically, sexually, and psychologically abuse their dating partners are more likely to espouse this ideology than those who are not abusive. Familial patriarchy is a discourse that supports the abuse of women who violate the ideals of male power and control over women in intimate relationships.[47]

In earlier times, North American law—the law of men—helped husbands prevent their wives from leaving them. Today, legal provisions are not as sexually asymmetrical, and men must rely on their own spouse-controlling resources to a greater degree. The use of violence as a means of social control escalates when marital/cohabiting partners separate, because separation is an extreme public challenge to male partners who believe they own their female intimate partners and therefore have the right to control them.[48] Eighty per cent of the 43 rural women who participated in my Ohio study stated that the male ex-partners who sexually assaulted them feel that "men should be in charge at home." Marie said that her ex-husband "wanted to be in control. He was in control for us, or you know I felt it." Moreover, like Joan's ex-husband, many of the interviewees' partners isolated them to maintain control:

> He didn't allow me to socialize at all. My place was at home
> with the children and that's where I was most of the time.
> The only thing I went out for was if they had a parent-teacher
> conference at school. I went for that. But no, I had no outside
> contact.[49]

Most of my respondents stated that they were raped during or after separation/divorce because their partners wanted to show them "who was in charge." Tanya was one of many interviewees who had a partner that was determined not to let her go:

> He did it because I was his and he felt he could. And it was his way of letting me know that, ah, first of all, of letting me know that I was his. And secondly, letting me know that, um, that I wasn't safe anywhere. And I, when we were together, when he had forced me to go back together with him, ah, he, ah… raped me as another form of, of possession. And I think also as a reminder of what could happen. And ultimately, at one point, I believed that he raped me as part of his means of killing my unborn child.[50]

If we accept some sociologists' argument that the marriage licence is a hitting licence,[51] then the logical solution to the problem of wife abuse is legal separation or divorce. However, as demonstrated here, in Chapter Two, and elsewhere, for many women, separation or divorce does not stop patriarchal men from hurting them; estranged male partners can keep showing up and their visits can be deadly. Alas, as Lundy Bancroft states, "The abuser's dehumanizing view of his partner as a personal possession can grow even uglier as a relationship draws to a close."[52]

SUMMARY

What is to be done about reducing the alarming rates of violence against women? Before people committed to enhancing women's health and well-being can adequately answer this important question, it is first necessary to identify the key sources or *risk factors* associated with such violence.

The main objectives of this chapter were to challenge individualistic or non-sociological theories of violence against women and to focus on three powerful sociological determinants of such violence. Of course, not all men abuse their female partners, but the ones who do are more likely to consume pornography, have patriarchal male peers, and have patriarchal attitudes and beliefs. Obviously, there are other factors that contribute to violence against women, such as stress, unemployment, and poverty. However, it cannot be emphasized enough that the best efforts to explain woman abuse focus on men rather than women. In the mid-1980s, two prominent researchers in the United States found only one variable out of 42 characteristics allegedly related to wife-victims that consistently discriminated between abused women and those who were not abused.[53] Their finding still holds true today, and it is consistent with the argument that any woman is a possible object of violence. What differs is not the woman, but the man.

FIVE

Why Can't Abused Women Leave Home?

*Most of us say that we do not understand people who
put up with abuse from a spouse or lover. Most of us
say that we would leave if that happened.*[1]

Thus far, this book has not presented much, if any, good
news. Still, it is important to remember, as noted in Chapter
Two, that most abused women eventually leave the men who
assault them, regardless of their relationship status (e.g., dating,
cohabiting, or marriage). In fact, close to 80 per cent of beaten
women in Canada, the United Kingdom, and the United States
flee harmful relationships. About 101,000 women and children
stayed in the 569 Canadian shelters for abused women in 2008.
In February 2009, the Calgary Women's Emergency Shelter
experienced a 30-per-cent increase in calls for help over the
same month in 2008.[2]

Nevertheless, throughout Canada and in other countries,
we repeatedly hear, "Why don't battered women just get up and
leave?" The following developments that have occurred since
the mid-1980s seem to have addressed the problem:

- increased awareness about woman abuse and more
  education programs;
- police training programs concerning woman abuse;
- police affirmative action hiring programs to increase the
  number of women officers;
- mandatory arrest policies;

+ a major increase in the number of shelters and transition houses;
+ a growth in programs to counsel batterers;
+ resources and services for children who have witnessed woman abuse; and
+ coordinated, community-based approaches to providing help to those abused.[3]

Legal decisions and relatively new laws have also made it easier for all abused Canadian women to leave violent homes, including:

+ the 1990 Lavallee Supreme Court Decision, which ushered in the use of battered women's syndrome defence;
+ the 1993 Criminal Harassment/Anti-Stalking Law; and
+ legislation allowing police to remove guns from a residence in which an occupant has been charged with threatening or assaulting another occupant.[4]

On the surface, these statistics, laws, policies, and initiatives look promising and/or effective. However, some mirror the factors that create woman abuse and do not target the broader social, political, and economic forces that contribute to this harm. For example, harsh law-and-order approaches often silence many women who are abused because they cannot tell their story in a traditional justice setting without being, or feeling, belittled. The battered woman syndrome defence typically relies on psychiatrists as credible expert witnesses in court, thus strengthening the idea that woman abuse is a medical or psychiatric problem. Increasingly, women who seek help for abuse-related mental health issues are having their support-seeking behaviour used against them in child custody and access cases.[5]

In sum, then, although abused women now have more resources to choose from, it is still not easy for many to leave, and they are not markedly safer when they do exit dangerous relationships. Indeed, as has been repeatedly stated in this book, separated/divorced women are at high risk of being killed by their estranged partners. Additional problems abused women and those struggling to help them face are:

+ challenges from patriarchal fathers' rights groups and others promoting an anti-feminist backlash[6];
+ a shortage of affordable housing and cutbacks to social service delivery[7]; and
+ joint custody or poor access arrangements forcing abused mothers into ongoing contact with abusers, thus creating safety issues, as they and their children have to deal with the controlling tactics of and emotional abuse by the perpetrators; in extreme situations, women or children have been murdered by these abusive men.[8]

A much longer list of problems and challenges abused women now face could easily be provided here, but the key point to consider is that some women clearly are trapped in abusive relationships. Hence, Sandra Horley suggests that our question would be best directed toward "what keeps her from leaving" rather than "why does she stay."[9] The issue is made more difficult by the fact that not all women or relationships are alike. It is also important to keep in mind Evan Stark's observation that

> Abused women are much less likely than the professionals whose help they seek to regard decisions about physical prox-imity as means to end abuse and much more likely to regard separation as a tactical manoeuvre that carries a calculated risk within the orbit circumscribed by assault or coercive control. The disjunction between what victims and outsiders expect from separation remains a major obstacle to effective inter-vention and communication in the field.[10]

WHY DOES SHE STAY?

Following an approach taken by Alyce LaViolette and Ola Barnett[11] to help sensitize readers to the complex array of rea-sons for why women stay in abusive relationships, I would like to ask you if you were ever involved in a romantic relationship and exited it, only to reflect on it and wonder why you stayed so long? If so, perhaps you, like many survivors of woman abuse, were either heavily invested emotionally and psychologically in the relationship, ideologically opposed to separation/divorce, or may have seen your partner as an emotionally dependent person who badly needed your warmth, care, and nurturance. Love is also a key factor in why abused women stay, leave, or return. These women don't want the *relationship* to end; they want the *violence* to end.[12] There are many reasons why women do not leave or why they return to abusive relationships, and some of the most salient ones are described below.

Fear

Stark observed that leaving an abusive relationship is a tactical strategy that carries a calculated risk. Some women are simply afraid to leave—often with excellent reason. They are convinced that they will be beaten and/or sexually assaulted if they stay but killed if they try to leave (see the intimate femicide section in Chapter Two). After living with violent men for years, they are often much better judges than outsiders of what their partners are capable of doing. Other women are afraid of being on their own, often because of a lack of resources: they just don't believe they can house and feed their children. They may have a problem of self-esteem after years of being belittled; they have come to believe that they are not capable of making decisions for themselves. Generally, however, as stated in the conclusion to Chapter Four, attempts to study battered women to see how they are "different" (e.g., low self-esteem, low intelligence, fewer economic resources, a history of violence in the family, personality differences) are rarely fruitful. An abused women is just like any other woman, except that she has been caught in a situation of frightening proportions.[13]

The Web of Emotional Abuse[14]

British feminist scholar, practitioner, and activist Catherine Kirkwood uses the concept of a "web" to explain how it is emotional abuse, not physical abuse, that ties women to these relationships.[15] Of course, physical abuse is also emotional abuse. How can one feel emotionally right after been beaten up? Rather than being constrained by a single thread, many women are caught in a web of factors, delicately interlaced and interconnected, that hold and trap them. No one strand can be isolated and viewed on its own; each receives support from the others. Further, this web is invisible, so that a person lacking knowledge of the dynamics of woman abuse may not necessarily see broken bones or black eyes.

The strands of the web are many and have been identified often in the literature. They may be the result of acts of an individual man, such as subjecting the woman to constant degradation and denigration; imposing a constant and never-ending fear that a beating may be coming at any time, day or night; cutting the woman off from any potential support such as friends, family, ministers, or doctors; forcing her to live in economic deprivation while the man always has enough money for his hobbies; and eventually creating emotional dependency, so that she has no outlets for joy or solace except her very oppressor. Or, as feminist literature has long pointed out, the strands of the web may be societal, based on traditional ideas that men should be superior in the family and that they have the right to enforce that tradition with violence.[16]

Unfortunately, in dealing with human beings, nothing is ever as simple as it looks. Analysis is made much more complex by the fact that some people are able to apply the scenarios outlined above to situations that do not seem to follow the proper script. For example, similar abuse occurs in lesbian relationships; a growing number of studies show that violence is found in these relationships as often as in heterosexual intimate unions. Lesbian abuse is marked mainly by one partner being extremely dependent on the other and thus feeling a need to use violence to exert power and domination over the other. Lesbians may be bound by a particularly sticky strand in that they may have even less support outside the couple than anyone else. Their relationship may be secret from family or employers; supports such as shelters or public services may be even less available to them than to other battered women; and the lesbian community itself may be too confused and embarrassed that this "male" disease has hit them to offer enough support.[17]

Other groups or individuals in society may have other strands that bind them. For example, according to one female Eastern Ontario public housing resident interviewed by DeKeseredy et al., 99 per cent of the women enrolled in a literacy program provided by a local community health centre were Somali women, and many of their husbands were opposed to this program because it challenged their patriarchal control. She also said that most of the abused Somali women who lived in her public housing community do not seek social assistance. Factors that make the web tighter for many immigrant/refugee women living in Canada are:

+ They do not trust the local police because of their brutal encounters with criminal justice officials in their countries of origin.
+ They have language difficulties and are worried that the police will turn to their husbands to explain what happened. Even when an interpreter is brought in, these women may worry that this person will misrepresent their concerns and needs.
+ They are less likely than female members of the dominant culture to know that woman abuse is against the law.
+ They fear that they will be ostracized by their families or communities for disgracing these groups by drawing their victimization to the attention of legal authorities.
+ Like some battered African-American women in the United States, they may be under enormous pressure from their communities to accept woman abuse and the explanation that it is caused by the men's stress of being the object of racism in the white community.
+ They may also resist calling the police because they do not want to subject their male partners to the racism and bias that they see as endemic to the criminal justice system.[18]

As one immigrant woman told DeKeseredy and MacLeod, "My people have been oppressed for centuries. My husband beats me because he has taken this oppression into himself. I cannot become one with our oppressors. I cannot turn my back on him and walk to them."[19]

The Spiral[20]

Catharine Kirkwood, who introduced us to the concept of the web, uses another metaphor that is just as helpful: the spiral. The strands in the spider's web are farther apart at the outer edges, where the fly finds it easier to escape. Toward the centre, however, the strands are tightly packed and work together to hold the fly in place. Kirkwood discusses factors that bring a woman spiralling toward the centre, making it more difficult for her to escape an abusive relationship. These include a lowered self-esteem, a lowered sense of self-identity, health changes such as significant weight gain or loss, or depression or a loss of hope. According to Kirkwood, "In other words, the use of emotional abuse and physical violence acted to reduce the resources on which a woman might draw to challenge her partner's control or leave an abusive partner."[21]

"Place Matters": The Plight of Rural Women[22]

Eastern Michigan University criminologist Gregg Barak correctly asserts that

> Academics and policy-makers alike...often focus too exclusively on the urban environment to the detriment of the rural environment, as well as on the plight of the minority battered women who stay rather than the majority of battered and unbattered women who leave and who ultimately appear to be subject to even a greater danger or higher level of violence than those who stay.[23]

Undoubtedly, rural crime, including violence against women in private or domestic settings, has ranked among the least studied social problems in criminology and sociology.[24] As

Joseph Donnermeyer, Pat Jobes, and Elaine Barclay put it in their in-depth review of rural crime research, "If rural crime was considered at all, it was a convenient 'ideal type' contrasted with the criminogenic conditions assumed to exist exclusively in urban locations. Rural crime was rarely examined, either comparatively with urban crime or as a subject worthy of investigation in its own right."[25] However, we now have a growing body of qualitative and quantitative data that tell a different story about rural communities from the one usually told by criminologists and the media. We begin by defining rural communities as places with small population sizes and/or densities that exhibit variable levels of *collective efficacy*, which is defined as "mutual trust among neighbours combined with a willingness to act on behalf of the common good, specifically to supervise children and maintain public order."[26]

Common images in fictional and non-fictional accounts of rural life portray a slower, more peaceful way of living, picturesque farms, main-street businesses that give personal service to long-standing customers, little school houses with dedicated teachers and equally studious pupils, and a police chief who knows everyone by their first name. Further, newspapers and other media often characterize rural people as being nicer to each other than urban residents are,[27] while at the same time they portray them as remaining "backward."

The mass media frequently present an inaccurate picture of the rural–urban divide. Contrary to what many people claim, rural people are not necessarily more likely to help people they know, including relatives, neighbours, or friends. Available data challenge myths about the "rural warmth and hospitality" perpetuated by some journalists and others who perceive "small-town folks to be nicer." In fact, many, if not most, rural people are very suspicious of "outsiders."[28]

Mass media also emphasize tight-knit communities, strong and peaceful family ties, and rugged individualism in rural areas but repeatedly ignore the plight of rural women who are beaten, raped, and abused in many other ways by male intimates on a daily basis. In fact, Statistics Canada surveys and data collected by other sources reveal that, overall, rural and urban Canadian women experience similar rates of violence,

BOX 5.1 The Sad Fate of Too Many Native Women

Twenty-six of the missing Aboriginal women turned up dead on Robert Pickton's pig farm. [By 2006, there were 27 charges of first degree murder against Robert Pickton; one charge was later quashed. For more information on these murders, see Cameron 2007.] The bodies of 321 others were found under bridges, in rooming houses, on rural roads, in their apartments. The remaining 173 are unaccounted for....

More than 50 Aboriginal women have disappeared since 1970. Most were younger than 30.

The facts are finally coming to light, thanks to the digging, checking, and collating of the Native Women's Association of Canada. It has just issued a comprehensive report entitled *Voices of our Sisters in the Spirit.*

Last week, Liberal MP Anita Neville called on the government to launch an independent investigation into the devastatingly high rate of violence against Aboriginal women and girls. "Their plight has been almost entirely ignored for far too long," she told fellow parliamentarians.

Helena Guergis, Minister of State for the Status of Women, responded on behalf of the government. She pointed out that her department is providing funding to the Native Women's Association for its research.

That's true, but the Conservatives are delivering the last instalment of a five-year grant made by the Liberals. More importantly, Guergis didn't address Neville's call for an investigation. She couldn't. That's Justice Minister Rob Nicholson's job.

The Liberals aren't faultless. Most of the women went missing on their watch. Organizations such as Amnesty International and the Elizabeth Fry Society tried to sound the alarm. But their reports prompted only statements of concern and studies.

Last fall, a United Nations human rights committee issued an urgent appeal to the Canadian government to conduct a thorough probe to find out how and why the justice system has failed so many Aboriginal women.

Ottawa isn't solely to blame. Provincial ministers have averted their eyes. The police have dragged their feet. And the media have made little effort to find out why Aboriginal women are violently assaulted four times as frequently as non-Aboriginal women.

A national inquiry is needed. The cycle of violence will not end until policy-makers understand how poverty, homelessness, poor employment prospects, policy indifference, and racism lead to miserable, truncated lives.

But public pressure is needed even more. The longer Canadians are silent, the higher the death toll will climb.

Source: Goar, 2009, p. A23.

but rural women experience some more severe types of violence.[29] Many Aboriginal women live in rural parts of Canada, and they are at very high risk of violence compared to non-Aboriginal women as described in Box 5.1.

In spite of this wealth of data, woman abuse in rural North American communities is perceived to be rare or isolated incidents. There are several reasons for this, including the fact that it is seldom reported to the police; when it is, law enforcement officials give it selective inattention. This type of response is not limited to rural areas. Many urban police officers ignore the plight of battered women and sexual assault survivors. Still, while there is a system of social practices that generally serve to dominate and oppress rural and urban women alike, it operates differently in rural areas. People in urban communities often complain of being anonymous and victims of an uncaring and mysterious policing system. In rural communities, violent men are more likely to be protected by an "ol' boys network." Women there know that the local police not only may be friends with their abusers, but also may refuse to arrest them because of their friendship.[30]

Rural communities have other characteristics that make it even less likely that women will report male violence and that preclude them from escaping abusive relationships, including the acceptance of stereotypical gender roles (e.g., it is the role of women to stay with their husbands even if they are mistreated), geographic and social isolation from social services or victim support, the absence of public transportation, and a lack of economic opportunities.[31]

Economic Factors

According to Article XXV of the UN Universal Declaration of Human Rights:

> Everyone has the right to a standard of living adequate for health and well-being of himself and his family, including food, clothing, housing, and medical care and necessary social services, and the right to security in the event of unemployment, sickness, disability, widowhood, old age, and other loss of livelihood.... Motherhood and childhood are entitled to special care and assistance.[32]

While few Canadians oppose this declaration, the reality is that many Canadian women and children are suffering financially. The poverty rate for women in Canada is always higher than that for men, with approximately one out of every eight females living below the poverty line in this, one of the richest countries in the world.[33] When a female server in a restaurant works for a wage that precludes her from eating properly so that the customer she serves can eat more cheaply, she is, in addition to making sacrifices for customers, going to experience alienation, social exclusion, and depression.[34] As the Canadian Feminist Alliance for International Action (CFAFIA) correctly points out, in Canada

> Minimum wage and social assistance are so low that women often have to choose between poverty and remaining in a violent relationship. A lack of economic independence can make it impossible for women to move, leave a job, or buy the security system that might keep them safe. Returning to school to upgrade and paying for child-care may be out of reach financially for economically vulnerable women. Inadequate provision of legal aid prevents poor women from seeking protection orders or altering custody or access agreements, putting them and their children at risk of further harm.[35]

As will be addressed in greater detail in Chapter Seven, full and decent employment helps battered women leave abusive male partners. Nevertheless, it is extremely difficult for some women to leave because of the abuser's volatile response to her departure.[36] As we saw in Chapter Two, a substantial number of separated/divorced women experience various types of abuse. Thus, policy-makers should not simply assume that employment and higher wages will lead automatically to safety. Some estranged husbands or cohabiting partners engage in "patriarchal terrorism" to humiliate their ex-partners and to make them lose their jobs. Often, violent means of "sabotaging work efforts" influence employers to fire women to avoid problems in the workplace and to protect co-workers.[37]

Other economic reasons for staying in or returning to an abusive relationship include:

- few job skills;
- limited education or work experience;
- lack of language skills in English or French;
- disability;
- limited cash;
- no access to a bank account;
- inability to find or afford child-care in order to get out to work;
- financial cost of court and legal proceedings;
- inadequate coverage by Legal Aid, since cases of abuse and custody are so lengthy and demanding that Legal Aid often covers only a limited number of sessions;
- not qualifying for Legal Aid and not being able to afford a lawyer.[38]

It can be financially devastating for women to exit relationships. One woman I interviewed in rural Ohio summed it up tersely: "Economically? I'm at the bottom of the food chain now."[39] Many Canadian women experience the same problem. The average family income before separation of 27 abused women who participated in a recent study conducted in Durham Region, Ontario, was $75,268. Their post-separation income markedly dropped to an average of $22,587.50, with 44 per cent of the sample stating that they were relying on social assistance for financial support and 52 per cent on family and friends.[40]

It is not only that many women endure physical, psychological, and sexual abuse before and after leaving their partners. In addition, many men economically abuse them. This is what happened to one woman I talked to in rural Ohio after she tried to leave her partner:

> He...actually tried to ruin me prior to us splitting up. He forged my signature on a document to the amount of the car loan. He had someone else come in, because he knew the dealer. So, I was put on there as co-owner without my knowledge and he stopped making payments, which really hurt my credit bad. He doesn't help us with money except for the child support that the gets taken out of his cheque. So, financially I have nothing now. And he stole $13,000 from some bank accounts for my kids' college.[41]

There are many other economic factors, including difficulties finding housing and being unable to buy children's clothes. However, financial problems are often related to inadequate social support services and an absence of collective efficacy in women's communities.

Absence of Collective Efficacy

The tolerance of woman abuse by local law enforcement and the general population varies greatly between different kinds of communities. The quality and quantity of services available for abused women also vary between towns, cities, villages, and the like. The result of these variations is an uneven distribution of community norms about woman abuse and of both informal and formal assistance available to survivors of male-to-female violence. Some communities are taking strong and effective steps to reduce rates of woman abuse, such as using media outreach, community visits, and sexual assault training for advocates.[42] On the other hand, when asked about their experiences in the family court system, many of the 27 abused women who participated in the Durham Region study mentioned above felt they were characterized as difficult, crazy, selfish, or uncooperative if they stood their ground on child custody issues. This was especially true for women who talked about their fears for their children's safety from physical and sexual abuse. Many of the women felt that their concerns about child abuse were not only dismissed but were used against them.

Collective efficacy in communities takes different shapes and forms and is not necessarily restricted to deterring or preventing crime such as woman abuse. Moreover, what may appear to outsiders as social disorganization is often "simply a different form of social organization if one takes the trouble to look closely."[43] Sixty-seven per cent of the 43 women who participated in a rural Ohio study of separation/divorce sexual assault reported on a variety of ways in which their ex-partners' male peers perpetuated and legitimated woman abuse.[44] Below is an account of how such an all-male sexist network and other symptoms of what Neil Websdale[45] refers to as "rural patriarchy" functioned to help stop a rural Ohio woman from leaving her abusive partner:

> Another time, after I finally got away from him and I was
> having these problems. I was, I was on drugs real heavy, um,
> and I was trying to get away from him. He was still calling
> me. This was just in the last nine months. Um, I called Victim
> Awareness in my town and, um, told them that I had been
> abused by him. Oh, they kept telling me that they were going
> to do something about it, and they never did. The one other
> time I went to Victim Awareness, they told me that, um,
> they were going to question the neighbours and stuff. And
> the neighbours said that, um, you know, they said that the
> neighbours didn't, didn't see or hear anything. So, they said
> I didn't have enough proof. Basically, nothing was ever done.
> He's a corrections officer in the town that I lived in, and he's
> friends with the sheriff and whoever else.[46]

This type of response is not limited to rural Ohio and occurs frequently throughout Canada. Such insensitive experiences with service providers often echo abusers' messages (i.e., that no one will believe her, that he can get away with it) and cause survivors to become distrustful. Many abused Canadian women are isolated from friends, relatives, and their community. Again, collective efficacy can take many shapes and forms, and often what is perceived as the "common good" may actually be behaviours and discourses that threaten the health and well-being of women seeking freedom from patriarchal oppression.[47]

Researchers, practitioners, and activists have long known that a woman's decision to leave a relationship may be long and complex.[48] She may simultaneously feel oppressed and trapped by an inability to leave a relationship immediately. This may be for financial or economic reasons, because she has been unable to make adequate arrangements to care for her children, or for a variety of other reasons. Nevertheless, many women defy men's patriarchal control by emotionally separating from them. Emotional separation, a major predictor of a permanent end to a relationship, is a woman's denial or restriction of sexual relations and other intimate exchanges. Still, emotionally exiting a relationship can be just as dangerous as physically or legally exiting one because it, too, increases the likelihood of male violence and sexual abuse exchanges.[49]

Different women react differently to abuse. Some carefully plan their escape. Some erupt in anger at what has been done to them, which could motivate a quick escape. For example, one battered woman reported:

> After 15 years of physical and mental abuse, I turned into "Lorena Bobbitt."[50] I had cajoled and done everything I could over the years to help my husband's weak self-esteem and finally one night I snapped. I grabbed my six-foot, 200-pound husband, flung him on the floor (all five-foot, 95 pounds of me). He was so shocked, he laid there and took it. It was a great triumph for my self-esteem and the realization that my husband was the one with the problem, not me. Empowered, I divorced him quickly before I changed my mind, and left Youngstown to be with my family where I could get support.[51]

Very few women, convinced that their husband will kill them if they try to leave, convert this anger and fear into a homicidal act. Thus, although some argue that battered women are in a state of "learned helplessness,"[52] where they are paralyzed into fear and cannot leave their situations, others argue that they are active agents of their own lives. They may be in a state of compliance like the hostages of terrorists who know that "doing what they are told" is the best way to survive. However, as Sandra Horley points out, when all of women's energies are focused on short-term survival, "They may seem submissive and passive, but in fact, in all sorts of often subtle ways, they fight back, they adopt survival techniques and actively find ways of coping."[53]

SIX

The Consequences of
Violence Against Women

> *Much can be learned from the intriguing and
> sometimes triumphant, other times frustrating and
> disheartening lives of the survivors of abuse.*[1]

Regardless of where and when it takes place, women targeted by male violence are changed forever. This is not to say, however, that all abused women become passive victims and are unable to lead healthy lives. As Linda MacLeod puts it, they may have been "battered," but they are not "beaten."[2] In other words, they become survivors with plans for the future. Nevertheless, women targeted by the harms described throughout this book experience a wide range of negative consequences, and so do their children. The destructive outcomes are immeasurable.[3] Carol, a rural Ohio survivor of separation/divorce sexual assault, said, "Right now, I'd have to say, sexually, I'm probably ruined. I don't ever want to have sex again with anyone. I have no desire to have sex with anyone."[4] Linda Baker and Peter Jaffe describe the impact of abuse on the child in this Canadian case:

> Katie and her young mother were held at gun point by her
> stepfather for over three hours one night during the past sum-
> mer. He debated aloud whether his partner would be punished
> more if he killed her or if he killed Katie. A traumatized Katie
> becomes anxious whenever separated from her mother or
> when faced with the need to return home. Home reminds
> Katie of this traumatic event and she overhead that her step-
> father will be released from prison next month.[5]

As well as those addressed in other parts of this book, there are many other injurious consequences of violence against women in intimate relationships. The main objective of this chapter is to expand the focus on key effects identified in the scientific literature. It is to the physical health consequences on women that we turn first.

PHYSICAL HEALTH CONSEQUENCES FOR WOMEN

The Ohio Domestic Violence Network tells us that, in the United States, "Domestic violence is a health care problem of epidemic proportions."[6] Given the statistics presented in Chapter Two, the same can be said about Canada. Leading medical experts in the field, such as those affiliated with the world-renowned Centers for Disease Control and Prevention based in Atlanta, Georgia, have identified the following as key immediate and long-term physical health consequences of woman abuse[7]:

+ suicide attempts;
+ chronic pain;
+ gastrointestinal problems;
+ cardiovascular disease;
+ substance abuse;
+ pregnancy resulting from sexual violence or loss of an existing pregnancy following sexual violence, as well as a wide range of reproductive concerns;
+ chronic or long-term impairment resulting in some restriction or lack of ability to perform a physical action or activity in the manner or within the range considered normal;
+ vision problems;
+ skin allergies;
+ anaemia; and
+ bronchitis or emphysema.

Many, if not most, readers are probably saying to themselves, "You forgot death." Indeed, many abused women are at high risk of being killed by their current or former violent partners, and the vast majority of intimate femicide cases do not "come out of the blue." Rather, most men who murder current or former partners had ongoing conflicts in their relationships, and many have a history of violence and jealousy and/or possessiveness.[8] Some battered women commit suicide, but, to the best of my knowledge, it is unclear exactly how many do so in Canada. Regardless of how a battered woman dies, the effects of her death are widespread. As Tanis Day and Katharine McKenna remind us, "The effect on children who grow up without their mothers because of acts of violence, often carried out by their own fathers, is terrible and unpredictable. Such acts affect everyone, creating an escalation in the level of fear all live with daily."[9]

Many physically and sexually abused women in Canada suffer from multiple physical health problems directly related to intimate violence.[10] Women harmed by such violence seek medical care more often than do non-victimized women, to such a degree that in Canada the measurable health-related economic cost of violence against women is roughly $1,539,730,387 per year.[11] This figure provides even stronger support for the widely cited claim that woman abuse in Canada is a major public health problem.

PSYCHOLOGICAL CONSEQUENCES

Not only does violence against women cause serious and long-term physical effects, it also does considerable psychological damage and, again, changes survivors' lives forever. The most immediate feeling most abused women experience after an assault is helplessness. Anger, anxiety, depression, fear, post-traumatic stress disorder (PTSD), and many other negative psychological reactions typically occur later.[12] In addition to experiencing one or more of these psychological problems, many sexual assault survivors experience long-term or even permanent sexual aversion. An intense mistrust of men in general is another common problem identified in the literature on the psychological consequences of sexual assaults in intimate relationships.[13]

Catherine, a university student Martin Schwartz and I interviewed about 13 years ago, is another person who deeply mistrusts men. Date rape is often considered a minor event that perhaps only the sexually naïve or the badly injured suffer from. Rather than allowing date rape to ruin her life, Catherine took classes in rape victimization, led her campus's Take Back the Night March, and was at the time of the interview active in both campus and local community politics. She told us:

> Well, I used to date a lot. I haven't dated anyone since....
> I mean, I broke up with my boyfriend and I haven't dated
> anyone, don't want to. Would rather go out with women.
> Although, I think I'm unfortunately more heterosexual than is
> really convenient. Yeah, I would like to do that, and right now
> I really don't want much to do with men, as far as romantic
> situations. But like I said, I think I'm too heterosexual to go out
> with women.[14]

Like all types of interpersonal violence, violence against women also causes considerable stress. An American Psychological Association Task Force discovered that physical and sexual assaults are under-diagnosed precursors to many women's psychological health problems. Violence-related stress is also known to cause temporary or permanent brain changes and other mental health problems such as confusion and poor test or exam performance.[15]

Many more examples of negative psychological outcomes could be offered here. Often, abused women experience these mental health consequences in conjunction with physical injuries and use alcohol and/or drugs to dull both physical and psychological pains.[16]

FINANCIAL CONSEQUENCES

As described in Chapter Five, leaving abusive men can be financially devastating for many women; Chapter Seven will offer some progressive solutions aimed at dealing with this problem. Earlier in this chapter we saw how expensive the health care consequences are. Other costs of violence against women in Canada include:

- the average annual cost per shelter for battered women and their children is about $364,000, which is over $135 million in total;
- factoring in volunteer labour, about $29,790,275 is required to operate rape crisis/sexual assault centres across Canada; and
- the cost of prevention and treatment initiatives, including public education, community outreach, and counselling is conservatively estimated to be $28,790,275.[17]

These relatively dated estimates were calculated in the early 1990s. I am not aware of more recent published estimates in Canada; however, it is fair to assume that the costs have likely increased. The economic cost of woman abuse in the United States is conservatively estimated to be $5.8 billion a year, although this statistic includes only medical and mental health expenditures, lost productivity, and lost lifetime earnings. There is no national estimate of the total cost of violence against women in either Canada or the United States, perhaps because it is impossible to determine.[18]

There are, however, some recent provincial figures on expenditures related to violence against women. The Ontario government's update of its *Domestic Violence Action Plan* lists the following:

- more than 70 women's shelters, second-stage houses, and community agencies that provide services for abused women and their children received an additional $3.5 million annually under the Transitional and Housing Support Program;
- funding for the Transitional and Housing Support Program is now more than $10 million annually;
- in August 2006, Ontario women's shelters received a $1.52 million investment in new infrastructure funding to create 20 new beds and renovate 77 shelter beds for abused women; and
- $4.5 million over 3 years was invested in local Domestic Violence Community Coordinating

Committees, which are in place in more than 30 Ontario communities.[19]

In sum, whether you realize it or not, lethal and non-lethal forms of violence against women are part of *your* life, directly or indirectly. These crimes affect your taxes and cost the country a substantial amount of money that could be saved if greater effort were devoted to enhancing women's health and well-being, as well as their children's quality of life.[20]

THE EFFECTS OF VIOLENCE AGAINST WOMEN ON CHILDREN

Women assaulted by their current or former male partners are often not the only ones hurt by violence. For example, 19 per cent of the 43 women who participated in my study of separation/divorce sexual assault in rural Ohio stated that their partners abused their children, and one woman believed that her ex-partner raped her as a means of killing her unborn child. This is what happened to Tina's daughter:

> He came back October of the same year for a so-called emergency visitation, and he was able to take my daughter away from me for eight hours even though the DNA had never been proven. And, when my daughter finally came back, she had severe diaper rash, smelled like cigarettes and alcohol, and had bruises right, right on her thighs and on her wrists.[21]

Some men do not hit their children or force them to have sex but behave in other ways that are sexually and psychologically abusive. Below is one example that involved the use of pornography shortly after this rural Ohio man realized that his wife was going to leave him:

> I walked into him masturbating in front of my children to *Penthouse....* There were naked pictures, well not naked, but pictures of me in a bra and underwear that he had stolen and had developed.[22]

As Tanya Conlin, Jane Chapman, and Rita Benson remind us in their training and resource manual *After She Leaves*, "Even if children are not the direct target of violence, they suffer from tremendous emotional abuse and possible neglect from exposure to it."[23] Given the following statistics, it is logical to conclude, then, that many Canadian children are suffering from exposure to woman abuse:

+ Statistics Canada estimates that children have seen violence or threats in 37 per cent of households where spousal violence occurred[24];
+ approximately 70 per cent of children who directly saw spousal violence saw or heard attacks on their mothers[25];
+ close to 50 per cent of women who took their children to Canadian shelters did so to protect them from seeing assaults on their mothers; 39 per cent did so to protect the child from psychological abuse, 18 per cent from physical abuse, and 5 per cent from sexual abuse.[26]

It is often said that children are "witnesses" to violence. As some leading experts in the field note, the term "witness" is highly problematic because it implies a passive role. In fact, children exposed to their mothers being beaten, psychologically abused, or sexually assaulted by their fathers "actively interpret, predict, assess their roles in causing violence, worry about consequences, engage in problem solving, and/or take measures to protect themselves or siblings, both physically and emotionally."[27]

Each child is unique, and the effects on children vary according to age, sex, and a host of other factors. Here, guided heavily by the work of Linda Baker and Peter Jaffe,[28] the potential consequences of woman abuse at different ages are identified. Some key effects on preschoolers are:

+ learning unhealthy ways of expressing anger and aggression;
+ attributing violence to something they have done;
+ learning gender roles associated with violence, victimization, and patriarchal ideology; and

- instability may inhibit independence and they may engage in regressive behaviours.

The key potential consequences for school-aged children (six to eleven years) are:

- becoming more aware of their own reactions to violence at home and of the impact on others (e.g., concerns about mother's safety, father being charged);
- becoming more susceptible to adopting rationalizations heard to justify violence (e.g., alcohol causes violence; victim deserved abuse);
- decreased ability to learn due to impact of violence (e.g., they are distracted); these children may not notice or may disregard positive statements or selectively attend to negatives or evoke negative feedback; and
- learning gender roles associated with intimate partner abuse (e.g., males as abusers, females as victims).

The potential consequences for adolescents are:

- family skills for respectful communication and negotiation may be poorly developed; transition to adolescence may be more difficult for youth and family;
- they may try to physically stop violence and may use increased size to impose their will by physical intimidation or aggression;
- they may become more embarrassed by violence at home, may try to escape violence by increasing time away from home, and may use maladaptive coping to avoid violence (e.g., drugs);
- they may have difficulty establishing healthy relationships and are possibly at greater risk of becoming involved in dating violence (e.g., may see boys as abusers, gender role stereotypes); and
- they may become more influenced by negative media messages about violent behaviour and gender role stereotypes.

In the course of describing the effects of woman abuse on children, it is not uncommon to hear many service providers, journalists, academics, and members of the general public refer to the *inter-generational transmission theory*, a type of *social learning theory*. Briefly, proponents of this theory maintain that male children are more likely to grow up to assault female intimates if their parents abused them or if they observed their fathers assaulting their mothers.[29]

The inter-generational transmission theory has some empirical support and is accepted across the political spectrum. However, as sociologist Murray Straus and his colleagues observe, it is wrong to "put the whole burden of violence on what is learned in the family."[30] Many people who were raised in relatively non-violent homes abuse their female partners and children. On the other hand, there are others who have directly experienced child abuse or have watched their fathers beat their mothers but who have never beaten their marital/cohabiting partners or children. While many children's violent fathers may be directly or indirectly teaching them to become wife beaters, their mothers may spend a substantial amount of time and effort teaching them that wife beating is wrong and that their future wives/cohabiting partners deserve to be treated much better.[31]

How a violent husband's behaviour affected male children and their treatment of women is explained by this Scottish woman:

> It had the opposite effect on the boys. It's had the effect I'd hoped for. I used to say to them, "I've had to spend my time telling you this," that this wasn't the right thing for men to do, that they hadn't to treat a woman like that. They should treat a woman the way they'd like their own sisters to be treated, you know.... So it did work, whether it was that or whether in their own inside they say to themselves, "Well, I'm no going to be like that. I've seen how my mother suffers. I'll no do that to any woman." I've tried to tell them, so I think it worked. They're hard working, safe, look after their money. They're just normal blokes. They never have any trouble. They wouldnae hurt anybody. I mean, they're very hale and hearty boys, and they're

well brought up. So I've won, you know, I feel a great—I've a great satisfaction in knowing that all the time I did spend trying to teach them the things that their father should have taught them. I've won in the end.[32]

Children are not "hollow beings who emulate whatever they see." Most of them have a sense of justice and fairness, and many are likely to regard wife beating as "bad" or "evil."[33] This is not to say, though, that the family is not a key "training ground" for woman abuse and child abuse. As we saw in earlier chapters, people also learn violence and other forms of intimate abuse from external sources such as pornographic media and male peers. While most male children may not grow up to beat their wives or common-law partners, a male child who experiences abuse at home is at high risk of engaging in bullying behaviour.[34] Although defining bullying is the subject of much debate, most studies use Norwegian scholar Daniel Olweus's offering,[35] which considers a person to be bullied when she or he is exposed frequently over time to hurtful actions by one or more youth, but does not include incidents where two children of similar strength are fighting. Olweus also asserts that bullying can involve direct verbal and/or physical attacks as well as exclusion.

SUMMARY

In his critically acclaimed book, Brian Vallée documents that in Canada and elsewhere, "The war on women has run longer than all of the conflicts of the last two centuries combined, including the Cold War. Only in the past 25 years has there been any significant movement to end the conflict."[36] Some of the key consequences of this war have been described in this chapter, and you can probably think of many more. One such effect that is rarely publicly discussed is how society has become accustomed to widespread violence against women. Marc Lépine, who murdered 14 female students at the University of Montreal on December 6, 1989, in what is now known as the Montreal Massacre, stated that he hated women, a feeling shared by many serial and mass killers (see Box 6.1). Those

---

BOX 6.1 **A Serial Killer's View of Women**

"I actually look good. I dress good, am clean-shaven, bathe, touch of cologne—yet 30 million women rejected me," wrote George Sodini in a blog that he kept while preparing for this week's shooting in a Pennsylvania gym in which he killed three women, wounded nine others, and then killed himself.

We have become so accustomed to living in a society saturated with misogyny that the barbaric treatment of women and girls has come to be more or less expected.

The mainstream culture is filled with the most gruesome forms of misogyny, and pornography is now a multibillion-dollar industry—much of it controlled by mainstream US corporations.

One of the striking things about mass killings in the United States is how consistently we find that the killers were riddled with shame and sexual humiliation, which they inevitably blamed on women and girls.

Life in the United States is mind-bogglingly violent. But we should take particular notice of the staggering amounts of violence brought down on the nation's women and girls each and every day for no other reason than who they are. They are attacked because they are female.

We would become much more sane, much healthier, as a society if we could bring ourselves to acknowledge that misogyny is a serious and pervasive problem, and that the twisted way so many men feel about women, combined with the absurdly easy availability of guns, is a toxic mix of the most tragic proportions.

Source: Herbert, 2009, p. 1.

---

who try to make the case for viewing Lépine's rampage as "an extreme instance of generalized violence against women" are often subjected to vitriolic verbal and written attacks by anti-feminists.[37] Bob Herbert asserts that the United States would be much healthier if its citizens acknowledged that misogyny is a serious problem.[38] The same can be said about Canada. How do we achieve this goal and how can we make Canada a safer place for women? Progressive answers to these important questions are provided in the next chapter.

SEVEN

"What Can We Do?": Policy Options

[I] know some things that women don't know about men.
By definition, women are never in all-male spaces. Women don't
directly experience what men say about them when there are no
women around. Women can hear these things second-hand, but it's not
the same as experiencing male-bonding/women-hating talk directly.[1]

Canadian women experience many "roadblocks to equality," such as sexual harassment in the workplace and in public places, forced prostitution, and other behaviours that are identified by scholars and activists as violations of their human rights. Violence against women not only is found in Canada, but also is "firmly rooted in cultures around the world." What, then, is to be done about this problem? This chapter will offer progressive answers that target broader sociological forces. However, it is first necessary to focus on the role of the criminal justice system, since many people believe that it should have the sole responsibility for dealing with all types of crime.[2]

CRIMINAL JUSTICE RESPONSES[3]

As in the United States, the Canadian criminal justice system during the past 30 years has introduced many new policies and practices to curb violence against women in intimate relationships, some of which are listed in Chapter Five. Prior to the early 1980s, many police officers were reluctant to charge woman beaters despite the fact that their violent behaviours were, and still are, violations of the law. Intimate male-to-female violence was not considered as serious as predatory street violence against strangers.[4] The major reasons for this differential enforcement of the law[5] were:

- the lack of explicit policies on making arrests and laying charges;
- negative attitudes toward intervening in "domestic conflicts";
- the perception that police officers are at great risk of physical injury when they respond to male-to-female violence;
- the frequent dismissal or reduction of charges in the courts; and
- the patriarchal ideology of male-dominated police departments.[6]

Feminist lobbying and education, empirical research, attitudinal changes among police officers, and growing public pressure on and interest within Canadian governments to respond to the needs of survivors of woman abuse have influenced many, if not most, police departments to take a more punitive approach to wife beaters. Arrests and charges are more common now, but despite government directives to the police to lay charges in all cases of wife abuse where reasonable and probable grounds exist, charges are still not typical. The same can be said about police responses to adult male-to-female sexual assaults in Canada, the United States, the United Kingdom, and other countries that have experienced much needed rape-reform laws.[7]

While legislative and policy changes were meant to send a strong message that woman abuse would not be tolerated, in some cases they resulted in counter-charging. In other words, when a woman called the police to report abuse and the police came to the home and charged her husband or partner, the man who was charged would accuse his wife of assaulting him and the police would be forced, under the "zero tolerance" policy, to lay charges against her as well. Unfortunately, many women who have no other choice but to use violence in self-defence to save their lives and/or those of their children are also arrested.[8] Consequently, as Susan Miller observes:

When women have fewer options (because they become reluctant to call police for help following enactment of these new policies), the emotional ramifications are costly: isolation is reinforced, as are their beliefs that there are no resources or that they are to blame. When women are themselves arrested, they do not call police during future abusive episodes, putting them at greater risk....[9]

Some feminists strongly supported aggressive criminal justice approaches to deal with woman abuse, seeking increased enforcement of existing laws and harsher penalties for convicted batterers. They fought legal battles and undertook consciousness raising to ensure that women who did seek assistance from the police would receive equal protection of the law, regardless of whether the perpetrator was a current or former intimate partner. However, as will be discussed later in this chapter, feminists have also been at the forefront of efforts to create holistic non-criminal justice responses to violence against women.[10]

Research and anecdotes on traditional justice system responses to woman abuse support the fears of feminists who are hesitant to recommend legal intervention. The system's emphasis on blaming, punishing, and taking the details of the abuse out of the context of the lives of those involved alienates and disempowers the battered woman[11]:

I don't recognize myself or my life in what the lawyers say about me. Even though they say that my case went well. I don't really see it that way. Everyone seems to think that because Roger was found guilty, and got a jail sentence, I won. I'm supposed to feel good about all this. I feel like a pawn in their game. Winning isn't for me, it's for them. Except that this is my life. All I wanted was for the police to stop the beatings. But I didn't bargain on all the meetings with lawyers, all the going to court that I've done. I didn't figure on the amount of time I'd be useless to my kids because I'd be so upset over something that a lawyer or a counsellor or someone else said, or because I'd have to go away from my kids to go to court or to meet with my lawyer. Maybe all the lawyers and the courts and the jail have put the beatings on hold, but it's put my life on hold too. I don't even know what my life is anymore. I don't know who I am. I'm the victim. Roger is the accused or some other stupid name. Allison and Casey are the children of a convict now. What happened to Roger and Louise and Allison and Casey? Will any of us ever get our lives back? Will we ever be just people, or will we always be somebody's "case"?[12]

Research has questioned the effectiveness of the criminal justice system as a way to protect women and to meet their needs. Early US studies emphasized the effectiveness of arrest, but this conclusion was based largely on the results of the Minneapolis Domestic Violence Experiment, in which researchers randomly assigned police to respond to domestic violence calls through arrest, which meant the offenders spent the night in jail; separation (i.e., the offender had to leave the house for eight hours); or counselling, including informal mediation in some cases. The results showed that men who were arrested were less likely to abuse their wives during a six-month follow-up period than men who were counselled or separated from their wives. The researchers concluded that arrest and incarceration alone will have a major deterrent effect.[13]

The effectiveness of arrest in deterring abusive men from subsequent violence was also supported by a study conducted in the 1980s in London, Ontario. It found that, according to police files and interviews with victims, there were significant reductions in abuse when charges were laid. Further, when charges were laid, the victims/survivors were more satisfied with the help received from the police. However, even the authors of the study cautioned that the results might not be replicated in other locations. They attributed at least part of the success of the mandatory arrest policy in London to the active way in which the city responded in a consistent, coordinated, and responsive matter to woman abuse.[14]

This warning has, through more recent research, proved to be well founded. In fact, we now have empirical evidence showing that arrest has a relatively small deterrent effect on woman abusers.[15] For this and other important reasons, some of the leading experts in the field now echo this argument made over 20 years ago: "[F]or those who are directly involved in responding to domestic assaults, it might be profitable to begin thinking about new or additional strategies for dealing with the problem."[16]

Other studies suggest that women do not feel that the justice system meets their needs and that people working in the justice system question the appropriateness of emphasizing a harsh "law-and-order" response to woman abuse. The bulk of the research on policies that emphasize the use of "get tough" approaches show that these initiatives often mirror the factors that contribute to abuse. For example, they make many women feel powerless. This is not to say, however, that the criminal justice system should be totally rejected, and it is important to note that arrests benefit many women because they set in motion means of assistance, such as shelters and counselling, that they would otherwise not have received or known about. Some criminal justice responses also have symbolic functions in the sense that they give male abusers the message that the harms they commit behind closed doors are deemed to be just as serious as those done by strangers on the street.[17]

These criticisms of the criminal justice system should not be construed as calls for decriminalizing woman abuse or for a return to the days when police had more discretion to make arrests. Yet criminal justice measures alone do little, if anything, to prevent woman abuse on a broader societal level. Additionally, most feminists today do not believe that the criminal justice system, regardless of its effectiveness, should have the sole responsibility for dealing with rape, stalking, wife beating, and the like.[18] This is a problem that University of California, Irvine, criminologist Elliott Currie refers to as compartmentalizing "social problems along bureaucratic lines."[19] Real life does not play itself out along the bureaucratic lines set up by government agencies. The federal minister of finance, who manages economic problems that contribute to violence against women in poor and socially excluded communities, rarely, if ever, considers how economic decisions could affect crime rates or discusses with the federal minister of public safety or police chiefs or officers economic issues, such as General Motors factory and dealership closures, the North American Free Trade Agreement

(NAFTA), or cuts in employment insurance. Consequently, many policies are adopted without taking into account the ultimate effect on woman abuse and other crimes. Thus, police, Crown prosecutors, prison officials, and other criminal justice personnel are called in to "clean up the mess" made by the rest of society.

A central argument of this book is that violence against women is a key symptom of structural inequality and that people who want to reduce or stop this harm must find progressive ways of eliminating social inequality while simultaneously meeting the unique needs of members of a diverse multicultural society. As Claire Renzetti, editor of the journal *Violence Against Women*, reminds us:

> Of course, while the causes of and solutions to the problems are not individualistic, but rather structural, we cannot lose sight of individuals. The challenge we confront is to disentangle the complex relationship between individuals and society, including our own roles in this dialectic. A tall order, no doubt, but the only one with a chance of real success.[20]

Regardless of their limitations, the aid of criminal justice officials is necessary in the ongoing and ever-changing struggle to end violence against women; therefore, criminal justice reforms are needed in addition to broader structural changes. Every advanced industrial society requires a combination of formal and informal processes of social control.[21] To improve police responses to sexual assault cases, feminist scholar and activist Susan Caringella suggests that high-ranking members of police departments should be required to keep summaries of the amount and types of sexual assault complaints, the percentage of unfounded complaints, the manner of the investigation, whether an arrest warrant was sought, and what charges were authorized. She also calls for making this information readily available through local media, in public meetings with the police, on websites, or on postings in police departments or courthouses.[22]

Below are some more progressive police reforms recommended by Canadian journalist Brian Vallée:

- In all violence against women calls, have a "without delay" response.
- Recruit more Aboriginal officers.
- Work with Aboriginal communities to develop protocols ensuring appropriate and effective responses to reports of missing Aboriginal women and children.
- Identify, monitor, and manage high-risk cases and vigorously enforce bail conditions arising from a violent offence or threat of offence.
- Institute a dedicated police unit that has links to community-based experts to deal specifically with high-risk domestic violence cases, to ensure an appropriate response.
- Train 911 operators and dispatch personnel in issues surrounding domestic violence, and provide them with prioritized questions to help them assess immediate risk to callers and first responders.
- Enter restraining orders into the Canadian Police Information Centre (CPIC) system immediately so that if there is a breach of law, there can be a quick police response under the Family Law Act.[23]

Such reforms are part of what some scholars and activists refer to as a "broader vision,"[24] one that targets the key social, cultural, and economic forces that motivate men to abuse female intimates, such as violent and pornographic media, poverty, racism, and unemployment. It is to some major elements of the broader vision that we turn next.

MOVING FORWARD, SAVING LIVES

Feminists and other progressives have called for coordinated, collaborative, community-based initiatives in what former Chief Justice of Ontario Roy McMurtry called a "multi-pronged approach" to dealing with woman abuse.[25] In the remaining sections of this chapter, I hope to stimulate your sociological imagination around such kinds of change. Much of what is suggested involves "reaching men."[26] Certainly, as Ron Thorne-Finch puts it, "since it is men who are the offenders, it should be men—not women—who change their behaviour."[27] However, it cannot be emphasized enough that many women across Canada are involved in numerous ongoing efforts to stop violence against them and their sisters. Such work often involves public awareness campaigns, Take Back the Night marches, fundraising for shelters, organizing memorials, electronic protests on Facebook, struggling for legislative changes, interviews with local and national media, and a myriad of other activities.[28]

Closely related to these and other strategies used by women's groups is the emphasis on partnership. The widely recognized need for collaboration has been highlighted over the past 30 years in many documents produced by activists, researchers, and policy analysts. For example, the *Final Report* of the Canadian Panel on Violence Against Women states:

> Building alliances across the issues that divide women will have to be given priority in the struggle to end violence against women. Patriarchy thrives on fragmentation and divisions. The existence of one oppression creates fertile conditions for the others. That is why all oppressions must be resisted together.[29]

Responding to Pornography[30]

It may seem painfully obvious, but it is worth repeating Susan Caringella's observation that "The media do a horrific job of sensationalizing crime, sex, and violence."[31] As described in Chapter Four, pornography is a central part of this problem and warrants considerable attention because it degrades, objectifies, and hurts men, women, and children in so many ways. It is also a major correlate of various types of male-to-female violence,[32] including sexual assault in dating relationships. One obvious way of dealing with pornography is to simply not view it, read it, or participate in any public or private events that involve pornographic words, behaviours, or images. Another strategy is to complain to hotel managers and owners about offering customers pay-per-view "adult films." I frequently travel and stay in hotels. Upon arrival at the front desk I often say to the clerk, "Your company is proud to offer a smoke-free environment, but you offer movies that harm women. I find this offensive and

would like to speak to the manager." The typical response I get
is something like this: "Well, Sir, it is your choice not to watch
it and what TV services we offer is beyond my control." After I
return home, my usual routine is to write a formal complaint.
Thus far, I have never received an official response.

Although it is important to take individual actions such
as mine, Robert Jensen is correct to point out that "It's not
enough for us to change our personal behaviour. That's a bare
minimum. Such change must be followed by participation in
movements to change the unjust structures and the underlying
ideology that supports them."[33] Informed by this philosophy,
one collective strategy that could make a difference is to take
the advice of a close friend of mine who works in the Ontario
provincial government. She suggested that organizations plan-
ning large conferences should make explicit in their negotia-
tions for discount group rates that they will not book rooms
in hotels that provide pornographic media. This strategy is
currently being used by the Minnesota Men's Action Network:
Alliance to Prevent Sexual and Domestic Violence and is referred to as the Clean Hotel Initiative.[34] Additionally, groups of
men and women should collectively expose and criticize injurious media coverage of woman abuse and boycott companies
that profit from pornography.

Such efforts might work because of their financial impact,
but they are also likely to be accused of promoting censorship.
Yet Canadians and citizens of other countries have managed
to express their disgust and dismay at even the slightest hint
of harm to animals in the movies. Where the plot line requires
an animal to be fictionally harmed (e.g., a horse and rider in
a Western accidentally fall over a cliff), film producers find it
essential to report in the credits that their set was inspected and
monitored by animal rights organizations. There are virtually
no movies that show animals burned, dismembered, stabbed or
shot to death, electrocuted, beaten or kicked, or raped. We save
these images for stories about men and women. Similarly, there
are no movies that depict positively the mass execution of Jews,
gypsies, and the mentally ill by the Nazis in World War II, nor
are there proslavery pictures showing approvingly how white
people beat, starved, and tortured African slaves to get them

to behave "properly." Anti-pornography educators and activists should insist that the same consideration should be given to depictions of violence against women as to violence against animals, Holocaust victims, and slaves.[35]

Men's Informal Responses to Abusive and Sexist Men

Because most Canadian men do not abuse women, we can assume that the average Canadian man is a "well-meaning man." According to Tony Porter, co-founder of the progressive coalition A Call to Men Committed to Ending Violence Against Women, a well-meaning man is

> a man who believes women should be respected. A well-meaning man would not assault a woman. A well-meaning man, on the surface, at least, believes in equality for women. A well-meaning man believes in women's rights. A well-meaning man honours the women in his life. A well-meaning man, for all practical purposes, is a nice guy, a good guy.[36]

However, well-meaning men also directly or indirectly collude with abusive men by remaining silent for several reasons, including those listed in Table 7.1.[37] I agree with Ted Bunch (also a co-founder of A Call to Men) who asserts that "When we remain bystanders we are making a choice to support the abuse. The abusive behaviour of any man reflects and therefore reinforces the established status and privileges of all men."[38]

Feminist men are distinct from well-meaning men. Although there are variations in the feminist men's movement, a general point of agreement is that men must take an active role in stopping woman abuse and eliminating other forms of patriarchal control and domination throughout society.[39] Feminist men place the responsibility for woman abuse squarely on abusive men. A central argument of this book (and that of others, such as Thorne-Finch's) is that one of the most important steps a man can take if he wants to improve women's quality of life is to join the feminist men's movement, which first involves self-examination and self-discovery.[40] In other words, men must be willing to examine their own attitudes and beliefs about

TABLE 7.1 Some Concerns Men May Have About Whether They Should Help Abused Women

Points of Concern	*Points to Consider*
You feel that it's none of your business.	It could be a matter of life or death. Violence is everyone's business.
You don't know what to say.	Saying you care and are concerned is a good start.
You might make it worse.	Doing nothing makes things worse.
It is not serious enough to involve the police.	Police are trained to respond and utilize other resources.
You are afraid his violence will turn to you or your family.	Speak to him alone. Let the police know if you receive threats.
You think she doesn't want to leave because she keeps going back to him.	She may not have had the support she needed.
You are afraid he will become angry with you.	Maybe, but it gives you the chance to offer your help.
You feel that both partners are your friends.	One friend is being abusive and the other lives in fear.
You believe that if he wanted help or wanted to change his behaviour, he would ask for help.	He may be too ashamed to ask for help.
You think it is a private matter.	It isn't when someone is being hurt.

women, sexuality, and gender relations. This is what Jackson Katz refers to as "similar to the sort of introspection required of anti-racist whites."[41]

Following this transition in their lives, newcomers to the feminist men's movement need to confront and openly talk to men who abuse women, even if they are friends, neighbours, or employers. Table 7.2 includes some of the warning signs of abuse to keep in mind.[42] It is also necessary to implement the

TABLE 7.2 **Major Warning Signs of Woman Abuse**

• He puts her down.	• She may be apologetic and makes excuses for his behaviour or becomes aggressive and angry.
• He does all the talking and dominates the conversation.	
• He checks up on her all the time, even at work.	• She is nervous talking when he's there.
• He tries to keep her away from you.	• She seems to be sick more often and misses work.
• He acts as if he owns her.	• She tries to cover her bruises.
• He lies to make himself look good or exaggerates his good qualities.	• She makes excuses at the last minute about why she can't meet you or she tries to avoid you on the street.
• He acts like he is superior and of more value than others in his home.	• She seems sad, lonely, withdrawn, and afraid.
	• She uses more drugs or alcohol to cope.

following or modified individual strategies suggested by Ron Thorne-Finch and Robin Warshaw[43]:

• Put a "Stop Woman Abuse" bumper sticker on your car and declare your home, workplace, recreational centre, or classroom a woman-abuse–free zone.
• Confront male friends, classmates, co-workers, teachers, and so on, who make sexist jokes or who engage in sexist conversations.
• Confront men who perpetuate and legitimate myths about woman abuse.
• Take every opportunity to speak out against woman abuse and other symptoms of gender inequality.

How should feminist men or other concerned citizens talk to a man who abuses his female partner? It is easy to suggest confronting such a person, but certain strategies are necessary, such as the following recommended by the Ontario Women's Directorate:

- Choose the right time and place to have a full discussion.
- Approach him when he is calm.
- Be direct and clear about what you have seen.
- Tell him that his behaviour is his responsibility. Avoid making judgemental comments about him as a person. Don't validate his attempt to blame others for his behaviour.
- Inform him that his behaviour needs to stop.
- Don't try to force him to change or to seek help.
- Tell him that you are concerned about the safety of his partner and children.
- Never argue with his abusive actions. Recognize that confrontational argumentative approaches may make the situation worse and put her at higher risk.
- Call the police if the woman's safety is in jeopardy.[44]

Teaming up with other men to implement collective strategies is another vital step. Criticizing and challenging the broader social and economic structures and institutions such as the pornography industry, the military, the media, professional sports, and the justice system are ways of recognizing that the most effective methods of prevention and intervention are at the social and cultural systems levels. Alcoholics Anonymous (AA) functions in a similar way. We know from many studies that one of the most powerful determinants of woman abuse is patriarchal male peer support. AA replaces pro-drinking peers with those who oppose drinking (social system intervention) and replaces pro-drinking norms, values, and beliefs with the opposite set of norms, values, and beliefs (cultural system intervention). Similarly, feminist masculinism replaces pro-abuse peers with anti-sexist peers and patriarchal norms, values, and beliefs with those that are feminist.[45]

Unfortunately, regardless of where they live, most anti-sexist men do not socialize with other males who are concerned about striving for gender equity. One of the key reasons for this is that most feminist men do not publicly identify themselves as such. Therefore, formal feminist men's organizations, such as the White Ribbon Campaign described below, should be invited to hold town-hall meetings in community centres and other settings where feminist men can get together and develop community-based individual and collective strategies to reduce woman abuse.[46]

The White Ribbon Campaign is a feminist men's movement initiated in October 1991 by the Men's Network for Change (MNC) in Toronto, Ottawa, London, Kingston, and Montreal in response to the Montreal Massacre (see Chapter Six). MNC drafted a document stating that violence against women is a major social problem, that male silence about violence against women is complicity, and that men can be part of the solution. The campaign's goals are to get men involved in the struggle to end violence against women, to raise public awareness of this problem, and to support organizations that deal with the brutal outcomes of male-to-female victimization. Each year one week prior to the anniversary of the massacre, men are encouraged to wear a white ribbon that "symbolizes a call to all men to lay down their arms in the war against our sisters." The idea has caught on, attracting much attention throughout Canada, the United States, and elsewhere.[47]

There are other advantages to working with groups such as the White Ribbon Campaign. One is that it helps feminist men "avoid reinventing the wheel" because, like many women involved in the struggle to end woman abuse, they are at risk of "burning out" or wasting their time and energy if they simply duplicate the work done by other progressive men's organizations.[48] Still, the ultimate question for many people is this: do the individual and collective efforts of feminist men really make a difference? Obviously, I think they do, but consider the following indicators of success:

- Research shows that campaigns that encourage men to hold other men accountable for their abuse are likely to be effective, while those that indiscriminately blame all men are not.
- Male friends and relatives of woman abusers can have a major impact on their behaviour by addressing the abuse directly and defining it as unacceptable.

◆ Communicating with men about the importance of condemning abuse and providing them with some advice on how to confront abusers in a way that does not jeopardize their female partners will eventually create an environment in which woman abuse becomes socially unacceptable.[49]

As pointed out elsewhere,[50] we know that feminist men and feminist male collectives *can* make a difference. More than a lack of knowledge, it is men's unwillingness to change that is problematic, especially men who gain from woman abuse. Many men are uncomfortable giving up patriarchal power and are more attracted to participating in the anti-feminist backlash. Others despise sexism and woman abuse but will not join the ranks of feminist men because they don't know how to respond or feel guilty or ashamed.[51] Feminist men know these obstacles. Regardless of how long it takes to get there, the long, hard feminist journey toward a truly egalitarian social order is worth it, and my colleagues and I encourage all men to become fellow travellers.

However, the journey must involve men from all walks of life. The insights of Aboriginal men, men of colour, lower-class men, men who are disabled, gay men, and men from other minority groups should be taken into account, as well as the insights of women who belong to these groups. Unfortunately, most feminist men's groups consist of men who are mainly white, middle-class, and heterosexual. Other groups may provide feminist men with insight, and thus, at every group meeting, "we should always be conscious of who is not there and that we are not hearing those perspectives."[52]

Economic Reforms

Giving women the economic tools to make life choices that do not involve abuse has, for years, been a goal of advocates for women who are abused. A higher minimum wage and access to full-time meaningful jobs are necessary first steps that are often opposed, especially by conservative members of the private business sector who fear that such reforms will hurt the economy. This is a myth documented by many studies, especially those conducted in Europe. Some also assert that waitresses, gas station attendants, shop clerks, and cleaning women are "unskilled" and that their credentials and training do not warrant a higher income. This, too, is a myth. As journalist Barbara Ehrenreich discovered while doing service work, even the lowest occupations require a tremendous expenditure of physical and mental energy.[53]

"Work hardening" initiatives need to be introduced to address the problem of abused women lacking job-related skills to obtain "decent paying jobs." Work hardening is a program that allows battered women to spend small amounts of time in work settings, with the time gradually increasing. Based on her own policy work and research, Jody Raphael maintains that "performing limited work activities allows the survivor to experience and develop her competency in a work setting or public arena."[54] It also builds women's self-esteem and broadens their social network.

Full and decent employment for both men and women will also reduce the rate of woman abuse in poor Canadian communities. There is a high concentration of unemployed men living in public housing, who often more strongly adhere to the ideology of familial patriarchy than their employed counterparts. As uncovered by several studies, if they cannot financially support their spouses and/or children and live up to their culturally defined role as "breadwinner," jobless men might be motivated to beat their intimate partners because their more legitimate routes to personal power and prestige have been removed.[55]

Unemployed men are also more likely to spend a great deal of time on the streets. Not only does this routine activity put them at greater risk of engaging in and being victimized by predatory street crime, it also increases the probability of being influenced by male peer-group dynamics that perpetuate and legitimate woman abuse. These men use sexual access and dominate women to maintain their self-esteem in the absence of work. Through interacting with each other on the streets, in parks, and in other public places close to their residences, they create an ethos encouraging sexual assault and other brutal patriarchal behaviours, including wife beating and violence against female ex-partners.[56] Thus, reducing unemployment is also an important method of targeting patriarchal practices and discourses that exist beyond family/household settings.

At the time of writing this chapter, creating more meaningful jobs and creating a higher minimum wage seem like daunting tasks, given the rapid disappearance of manufacturing jobs in Ontario and other parts of Canada. Hence, to prevent the unemployment rate from skyrocketing, some sociologists suggest strategies such as job rationing; making earlier retirement a condition of employment; and ensuring that government, industry workers, and their representatives cooperate to shorten the work week, thereby increasing employment opportunities for those currently experiencing unemployment or underemployment.[57]

The Role of Government

On June 1, 2009, the Canadian federal government and the Ontario provincial government announced that they were extending a loan of US$9.5 billion of taxpayers' money to General Motors of Canada (GM).[58] Obviously, the well-being of GM and its workers was a much higher priority for these governments than preventing woman abuse. We saw in Chapter Two that Prime Minister Stephen Harper has cut funding to the National Association of Women and the Law; the amount of money this agency received annually ($300,000) pales in comparison to the sum given to "bail out" GM. And, as stated in Chapter One, Status of Women Canada was deemed by the Harper government to be no longer eligible for funding for advocacy, government lobbying, or research reports. Throughout Canada, we are witnessing increases in post-secondary school tuition, the closing of hospitals and schools, and the increasing elimination of public responsibility for a variety of social services.

Supporters of cuts to women's groups, to the services they provide to abused women, and to welfare and other parts of Canada's social safety net claim that alternative policies like those suggested in this chapter cannot work because they require too much money, which should be used to lower the deficit. If money has not been too tight to help GM and to build five relatively new correctional facilities for women, then money can easily be found for the solutions recommended here, if that is what people want. Government spending is always directly related to political priorities. What we need now is a fundamental readjustment in thinking about these priorities.[59]

The results of many studies point to the effects of inadequate government funding for the basic needs and services that could enable abused women to separate from their abusers more easily and safely, including but not limited to:

+ housing subsidy and refurbishment programs;
+ higher income support;
+ affordable, quality child care;
+ affordable and efficient public transportation;
+ increased access to emergency support and resources for survivors;
+ long-term aid to assist abused mothers in the transition to independence; and
+ increased income eligibility for legal aid.[60]

Government-sponsored "one size fits all" methods are not likely to help many women with special needs or circumstances or the practitioners who work with abusive men from different socioeconomic backgrounds.[61] As University of Kentucky researcher T.K. Logan and her colleagues observe, "creative solutions must be developed in order to serve women with victimization histories within the context of the specific communities where these women live."[62] Those who live in remote rural parts of Canada do not need to be reminded that cars are not luxuries in these areas but are essential for women's safety and for transport to child care, employment, and support services. Public transportation is not often provided in rural communities, although governments do subsidize urban bus, subway, and light-rail fares. Thus, in rural communities, an equal amount of money should be allotted for people who need cars. Likewise, more government money should be devoted to paying the transportation costs of rural advocates who spend much time on the road in their efforts to prevent violent assaults on women and children.[63]

Thousands of women living in Canada have special needs and/or concerns, and they have challenged existing approaches to violence against women. As Linda MacLeod and Maria Shin uncovered in their study of women who are abused and who speak neither English nor French:

> ...[they] do not even consider looking for help to stop their abuse, because the help that is available is not only usually linguistically and culturally foreign, but it often takes away the very things that give them strength. So, for example, the emphasis of many available services on short-term dependency on welfare is experienced as robbing women of dignity by eroding their value of self-sufficiency. Counselling approaches which do not emphasize practical approaches are seen by many women as all talk and no substance, as inappropriate personal intrusion by outsiders, and as patronizing.[64]

For all these reasons, government-sponsored service providers need to be educated about diversity issues, such as the historical trauma and unresolved grief that many Aboriginal people experience as consequences of European domination, genocide, cultural genocide, and forced assimilation. Many Aboriginal women and women from minority cultures reject a strictly secular approach to intervention or prevention and insist that their spiritual needs and faith traditions be woven into holistic responses that address their needs and uphold their strengths.[65]

Targeting the Mainstream Media[66]

Much has already been said about pornography, which is increasingly becoming mainstream in our society.[67] Belief in gender inequality is also promoted by elements of popular culture, such as Hollywood movies, video games, and certain genres of music, advertising, and television shows. Patriarchal violent messages transmitted by the media tend to increase people's tolerance for sexist discourses and practices, including violence against women in post-secondary school dating. Gangsta rap, a type of music with broad appeal among college and university students and other youth, sends out strong messages about the way to treat women and the need for an abusive patriarchal masculinity. Relationships are also characterized in many gangsta rap songs as unions in which men must dominate and control women.[68]

Patricia Hill Collins views rap as one of the contemporary "controlling images" used to oppress black women, and Oliver contends that rap's patriarchal or sexist lyrics "provide justifications for engaging in acts of violence against black women." Still, Weitzer and Kubrin assert that such music is a method of controlling all women because it is consumed by a diverse range of youth. In one experiment, youth who were exposed to rap music later reported a higher probability that they would engage in violence than those who were not so exposed. Other forms of popular music also promote violence as the appropriate method of maintaining patriarchal control. While these messages are aimed mainly at males, women growing up in the same society hear the same messages. Thus, some research has found that among female African-American adolescents, those exposed to violent rap videos are more likely to accept teen dating violence committed by a male.[69]

What, then, is to be done? According to leading experts in the field, media that glorify and legitimate any type of violence should be eliminated.[70] This is not going to be an easy task. Again, accusations of promoting censorship will have to be met by the educational approaches described above. People should organize mass boycotts of popular violent video games like *Grand Theft Auto*; parents, school teachers, and other adults in positions of authority and leadership should carefully monitor youth's use of electronic entertainment equipment and have frequent discussions with children about the harmful effects of violent media. However, stern lectures and restricting a child's access "can backfire. The 'forbidden fruit' can become more attractive."[71]

The Human Rights Approach

International documents do not treat male-to-female violence as a unique social problem, but, rather, link it to other forms of violence and structural violations against women.[72] This perspective is clearly stated in the paragraph quoted below from a UN report prepared for the Fourth World Conference on Women, held in Beijing, China:

> Violence against women both violates and impairs or nullifies the enjoyment by women of human rights and fundamental freedoms. Taking into account the Declaration on the Elimination of Violence against Women and the work of the Special Rapporteurs, gender-based violence, such as battering and other domestic violence, sexual abuse, sexual slavery and exploitation, and international trafficking in women and children, forced prostitution and sexual harassment, as well as violence against women, resulting from cultural prejudice, racism and racial discrimination, xenophobia, pornography, ethnic cleansing, armed conflict, foreign occupation, religious and anti-religious extremism, and terrorism are incompatible with the dignity and the worth of the human person and must be combated and eliminated.[73]

Such international documents equate woman abuse with a violation of human rights. They emphasize multifaceted, preventive measures that go beyond a focus on abuse to a broader emphasis on improving the position of women in society.[74] One manual prepared by an international group of experts included a list of measures that might be included in a prevention strategy, such as:

+ reforming the law to foster equality;
+ reforming the law to prohibit corporal punishment;
+ promoting equal opportunities and human rights; and
+ combating stereotypes in the media.[75]

In spite of such international emphasis on woman abuse as a hate crime and a violation of women's human rights, many people around the world refuse to accept that human rights standards are universal when applied to women because their culture and religion legitimate violent behaviours.[76] Nevertheless, there is a strong international women's rights movement, and many Canadian women are actively involved in it (see Box 7.1).

SUMMARY

Violence against women is a constantly evolving and never-ending social issue.[77] Many countries, including Canada, are once again at a turning point in their understanding and responses to wife beating, femicide, sexual assault, and the like. Approaches to prevention and control are changing as some existing services lose their funding; as questions are raised about the effectiveness of the criminal justice system and the battered women's shelter approaches that have been at the centre of responses to woman abuse since the 1970s; as new groups and individuals join those working to end abuse; and as more people from around the world exchange experiences about different approaches to prevention.

One of the major obstacles in the search for effective policies is the fact that there are many bad ideas and simplistic solutions; relying solely on the criminal justice system is a prime example of a bad idea. A large body of research has failed to generate conclusive evidence that incarcerating many people leads to major reductions in crime. Although the criminal justice system can help improve women's health and safety, it is only one part of the solution. It is time that we move the discussion of preventing woman abuse into the realm of social and economic policy.[78]

The progressive solutions suggested here constitute just the tip of the iceberg. I could have provided many more promising initiatives, including school-based education programs aimed at building healthy intimate relationships. However, one of the most important points to consider here is that decades of research, policy analysis, and work done by front-line practitioners tell us that social policy initiatives must use patriarchy in all its shapes and forms as a major frame of reference.

Undoubtedly, gender equality in the workplace, family, schools, athletics, and so on will enhance the well-being and health of Canadian girls and women.[79]

BOX 7.1 Hate Laws: Protection for Females Demanded

A coalition of students, academics, and educators is appealing to federal politicians to change the Criminal Code so [that] females are protected under hate laws.

In an open letter to Prime Minister Stephen Harper and opposition party leaders Stephane Dion, Jack Layton, and Gilles Duceppe released yesterday, the Violence in the Media Coalition urges them to "address a vital public safety issue affecting half of the population of Canada that can no longer be ignored."

Currently, the hate law covers individuals by colour, race, religion, ethnicity, and sexual orientation.

"Omitting girls and women from the list compromises their safety," the letter says. "There is no justification for it. It is a stark piece of unfinished business and one has to seriously wonder why it is taking so long to deal with it."

Peter Jaffe, of the University of Western Ontario and the group's spokesperson, said the coalition has been trying unsuccessfully to get politicians' attention.

"We wrote the open letter to the federal leaders hoping they'd work together on this."

Jaffe said two recent reports on the sexual harassment and assaults that young females encounter in Ontario high schools is a sign of the negative impact hateful images can have in the media.

"Whether you are looking at video games or music videos or if you look at pornography...there are more violent images and you begin to think these are acceptable ways to treat women," he said.

Source: Rushowy, 2008, p. A19.

Notes

Chapter One

1. This chapter includes modified sections of work published previously by DeKeseredy 2009a, 2009b; and DeKeseredy & Schwartz, 2011.

2. Muehlenhard et al., 1992, p. 24.

3. Elias, 1986, p. 4.

4. DeKeseredy, 2011; Smith, 1988.

5. Mills, 1956.

6. Tower, 2002; Alvarez & Bachman, 2008.

7. Becker, 1973, p. 9.

8. DeKeseredy, Ellis, & Alvi, 2005.

9. DeKeseredy & Schwartz, 2001.

10. Kilpatrick, 2004, p. 1218.

11. DeKeseredy & Dragiewicz, 2009.

12. Dutton, 2006.

13. Denham & Gillespie, 1999.

14. Ellis & DeKeseredy, 1996; Meloy & Miller, 2011.

15. Stanko, 1985; Ellis, 1987.

16. Gallaway, cited in Farrell, 2002, p. 2; for more information on this study, see DeKeseredy & Schwartz, 1998.

17. Dutton, 2006.

18. Fox, 1993, p. 322.

19. Kelly, 1994.
20. Schur, 1984, p. 10; for violence as bi-directional, mutual, or sex symmetrical, see DeKeseredy & Dragiewicz, 2009; for gender not as a major determinant of violence against women, see Anderson, 2005; for the difference between gender and sex, see Dragiewicz, 2009.
21. AuCoin, 2005; Mihorean, 2005.
22. See Johnson, 1996, for more information on this study.
23. Dutton, 2006.
24. Meloy & Miller, 2011; Schwartz, 2000; Brownridge, 2009; Mihalic & Elliot, 1997.
25. DeKeseredy, 2000; Jiwani, 2000.
26. Fekete, 1994.
27. Duffy & Momirov, 1997,
28. Cited in DeKeseredy & Schwartz, 2009, p. 49.
29. Pitts & Schwartz, 1993, p. 396.
30. Smith, 1994, p. 110; for underreporting, see DeKeseredy, 2000; for underestimating the amount of abuse, see Walby & Myhill, 2001.
31. Ellis, 1987; Adams et al., 2008.
32. Follingstad et al., 1990.
33. DeKeseredy & Schwartz, 2009, p. 83.
34. Bachar & Koss, 2001; Meloy & Miller, 2011.
35. Russell, 1990, p. 383.
36. Bergen, 1996.
37. DeKeseredy & Schwartz, 2009, p. 24.
38. DeKeseredy, et al., 2006; Kernsmith, 2008; Stark, 2007.
39. DeKeseredy & MacLeod, 1997, p. 5.
40. Duffy & Momirov, 1997.
41. For the US National Violence Against Women survey and criticisms of it, see Tjaden & Thoennes, 2000, and DeKeseredy, Rogness, & Schwartz, 2004; for Statistics Canada's 1993 Violence Against Women Survey, see Johnson, 1996; for the CNS, see DeKeseredy & Schwartz, 1998.
42. Saltzman et al., 1999.
43. DeKeseredy & Schwartz, 2001.
44. Hall, 1985.
45. DeKeseredy & MacLeod, 1997.
46. Fitzpatrick & Halliday, 1992, p. 76.
47. DeKeseredy & Schwartz, 1998.
48. Smith, 1987.

Chapter Two

1. The introduction to this chapter includes modified sections of work published previously by DeKeseredy, 2009c.

2. These are the words of an Ontario woman living in the Durham Region. She was abused before and after she left her male partner, and she lacked adequate legal representation. Her experiences and those of other women in similar situations are described in Dragiewicz & DeKeseredy, 2008.

3. Simpson, 2000, p. 95.

4. Grabb & Curtis, 2005; Hatt, Caputo, & Perry, 1990.

5. Grabb & Curtis, 2005.

6. The Act received Royal Assent on February 28, 2008. Its main measures are automatically refusing bail to people charged with gun crimes; making it easier for police to charge people driving under the influence of drugs; raising the legal age of sexual consent to 16 from 14; making it easier to prosecute and indefinitely incarcerate "dangerous offenders" after three convictions for serious crimes; and mandatory prison sentences for drug dealers. Three-strikes sentencing was first passed in Washington State in 1993 and was incorporated into federal US law in the 1995 Violent Crime Control and Law Enforcement Act. Under three-strikes laws, people convicted of three felonies are given sentences of life imprisonment with no possibility of parole for a very long time. At the time of writing this chapter, 26 US states had three-strikes legislation. For more information on three-strikes laws, see Jones & Newburn, 2002.

7. Contenta et al., 2008.

8. In 1994, the US Congress passed VAWA, which is what the late senator Paul Wellstone and his wife Sheila called "the most comprehensive anti-violence legislation to date" (2001, p. ix). Congress reauthorized VAWA in 2000 and 2005. The Act created new penalties for gender-related violence and new grant programs to motivate states to address physical violence against women and sexual assault.

9. Dragiewicz, 2008, p. 130.

10. Hammer, 2002, p. 28; Independent Women's Forum, 2002, p. 1.

11. See DeKeseredy & Schwartz, 2003; Carastathis, 2006.

12. DeKeseredy, 2009b.

13. DeKeseredy, 2009c.

14. CBC News, 2010; Angus Reid Global Monitor, 2008.

15. Cross, 2007, p. A8.

16. Kettani, 2009.

17. Corry, 1801.
18. Ellis & DeKeseredy, 1997.
19. Vallée, 2007.
20. Pottie Bunge, 2002, p. 1.
21. Polk, 2003, p. 134; for rates of spousal homicides, see also Kowalski, 2006.
22. DeKeseredy & Joseph, 2006, p. 307.
23. Cross, 2007; Domestic Violence Death Review Committee, 2004, 2005, 2007; Dauvergne & Li, 2006.
24. Ogrodnik, 2008; Elizabeth Fry Society, 2009.
25. Gartner, Dawson, & Crawford, 2001.
26. DeKeseredy & Flack, 2007; for more information on this exercise, see Katz, 2006, p. 3.
27. DeKeseredy & Flack, 2007.
28. Steven Lewis, cited in Vallée, 2007; Katz, 2006, chapter 9.
29. DeKeseredy, 2009b; DeKeseredy, Perry, & Schwartz, 2007.
30. For more information on hate-motivated violence against women, see DeKeseredy, 2009d.
31. Katz, 2006, p. 1.
32. For in-depth reviews of this literature, see DeKeseredy, 2009b, and Schwartz & DeKeseredy, 1997.
33. DeKeseredy, 2009b.
34. Johnson, 1996; Mihorean, 2005.
35. Native Women's Association of Canada, 2008; Sokoloff & Dupont, 2005; DeKeseredy et al., 2003; Jasinski et al., 2010.
36. Alvi 2009a, p. 301.
37. This section includes revised sections of work published previously by DeKeseredy, 2007.
38. Fagen, 2005.
39. Brownridge, 2009.
40. Dragiewicz & DeKeseredy, 2008, p. 22.
41. DeKeseredy, 2009b.
42. Gartner, Dawson, & Crawford, 2001; Wilson & Daly, 1994; Stark, 2007; Stout, 2001; Block, 2000; Russell, 2001, p. 176.
43. Johnson & Sacco, 1995; Mihorean, 2005.
44. Stark, 2007, p. 116.
45. DeKeseredy & Schwartz, 1998.
46. Kimmel, 2008, p. 45.
47. Connell, 1995; DeKeseredy & Schwartz, 1998.
48. DeKeseredy & Schwartz, 1998; Price et al., 2000.
49. Menard, 2001, p. 708.
50. Brownridge, 2009; Brownridge & Halli, 2001.

51. DeKeseredy, Alvi, & Schwartz, 2006.

52. Rennison & Welchans, 2000; Edin, 2000; Adams & Coltrane, 2005; Benson & Fox, 2004; Raphael, 2001a; DeKeseredy, 2007; Raj et al., 1999; Raphael, 2001a, p. 454.

53. DeKeseredy & Schwartz, 2009; Johnson, 1997; DeKeseredy, 2007; Raphael, 2001a; Adams & Coltrane, 2005; Edin, 2000; DeKeseredy & Schwartz, 2002.

54. DeKeseredy, 2007; Gumus, 2006; Tolman & Bennett, 1990); Schwartz et al., 2001.

55. Sokoloff & Dupont, 2005.

56. DeKeseredy et al., 2003.

57. Brownridge, 2009; DeKeseredy & Schwartz, 2009; Brzozowski, Taylor-Butts, & Johnson, 2006; Johnson, 2006.

58. DeKeseredy, Schwartz, & Alvi, 2000.

59. DeKeseredy & MacLeod, 1997.

60. Jasinski et al., 2010.

61. Statistics Canada, 2010.

62. Brownridge, 2009.

63. Guggisberg, 2010; Shoener, 2008; Garcia-Moreno et al., 2005.

64. Johnson, Ollus, & Nevala, 2008; Krug et al., 2002; Mujica & Ayala, 2008; Sev'er, 2008; Silvestri & Crowther-Dowey, 2008; Watts & Zimmerman, 2002; Proudfoot, 2009a.

Chapter Three

1. DeKeseredy & Joseph, 2006, p. 305.

2. Katz, 2006, p. 21.

3. Katz, 2006, p. 91.

4. Personal communication, June 21, 2005.

5. This section includes revised parts of material published previously by DeKeseredy & MacLeod, 1997.

6. See, for example, Swan & Snow, 2006.

7. For example, Straus, 1993.

8. Straus, 1979.

9. Smith, 1987, p. 177.

10. DeKeseredy & Dragiewicz, 2007; Dobash et al., 1992.

11. Mihorean, 2005.

12. For example, Statistics Canada, 2002.

13. Steinmetz, 1977–78.

14. Dutton, 2006, p. ix.

15. DeKeseredy, 2007; DeKeseredy & Dragiewicz, 2007; DeKeseredy & MacLeod, 1997.

16. For more information on this case, see Johnson, 1996; Comack, 1993; and *R. v. Lavallee*, 1990.

17. Goodmark, 2008, pp. 76–77.

18. DeKeseredy, 2009b; DeKeseredy & MacLeod, 1997; Jiwani, 2000.

19. DeKeseredy & Dragiewicz, 2007; DeKeseredy, 2006.

20. Straus et al., 1996.

21. DeKeseredy & Dragiewicz, 2007.

22. Christensen, 2002; Pearson & Gallaway, 1998, p. 81.

23. Dutton, 2006, p. 153.

24. Statistics Canada's 1993 Violence Against Women Survey was heavily informed by feminist scholarship. For in-depth information on the methods used in this study and the results generated by it, see Johnson, 1996.

25. DeKeseredy, 2009c.

26. Dutton, 2006, p. ix.

27. Gallaway, cited in Cobb, 1998, p. A3.

28. Schwartz & DeKeseredy, 1994.

29. Pearson, 1997.

30. Hickey, 2005.

31. Garbarino, 2006; Alvi, 2009b; Chesney-Lind & Irwin, 2008.

32. Chesney-Lind & Eliason, 2006, p. 37.

33. DeKeseredy, 2010.

34. Cohen, 1980; Ellis, 1987, p. 199; Schissel, 1997, p. 51.

35. Males, 2010.

36. Faith, 1993.

37. Olsson, 2003.

38. Currie, 2004, p. 14.

39. Glassner, 1999; Schwartz & DeKeseredy, 2008; Silvestri & Crowther-Dowey, 2008.

40. This section includes revised sections of work published previously by DeKeseredy & Dragiewicz, 2009.

41. Johnson, 2008.

42. Cited in National Institute of Justice, 2000, p. 2.

43. Johnson, 2008, p. 12.

44. Stark, 2006, p. 1024.

45. Pence & Dasgupta, 2006; Dasgupta, 2002; Bonisteel & Green, 2005.

46. Dutton, 2006, p. 98.

47. Schwartz & DeKeseredy, 1994.

48. DeKeseredy & Dragiewicz, 2009.

Chapter Four

1. Bancroft, 2002, pp. 8–9.
2. DeKeseredy & Schwartz, 1996; Gelles & Straus, 1988.
3. DeKeseredy et al., 2006, pp. 239–40.
4. Gondolf, 1999, p. 1; Gelles & Straus, 1988.
5. Gayford, 1975; Stark, 2007.
6. Bograd, 1988.
7. Bumiller, 2008.
8. Gelles & Cavanaugh, 2005, p. 188.
9. Zilbergeld, 1983, p. 32.
10. Dobash & Dobash, 1992.
11. Romito, 2008, p. 72.
12. Hunnicutt, 2009.
13. DeKeseredy & Schwartz, 1996.
14. Mills, 1959, p. 9.
15. Stanko, 1990, p. 85.
16. Russell, 1998, p. 3.
17. Jensen, 2007; Funk, 2006; Zerbisias, 2008.
18. Jensen, cited in Gillespie, 2008, p. A3.
19. Funk, 2006, p. 165.
20. Jensen, cited in Katz, 2006, pp. 188–89.
21. Jensen, 2007, p. 17.
22. See DeKeseredy & Olsson, 2011; DeKeseredy & Schwartz, 1998, 2009.
23. DeKeseredy & Schwartz, 2009.
24. Bergen & Bogle, 2000.
25. Russell, 1998, p. 150.
26. See DeKeseredy & Schwartz, 2009.
27. See DeKeseredy, 1990; DeKeseredy & Schwartz, 2009.
28. Funk, 2006; DeKeseredy & Olsson, 2011.
29. Sanday, 1990, p. 129.
30. DeKeseredy et al., 2006, pp. 241–42.
31. Warr, 2002.
32. Bowker, 1983.
33. DeKeseredy & Schwartz, 1998; DeKeseredy et al., 2003.
34. Wilson, 1996; Miller, 2008; DeKeseredy & Schwartz, 2009; Websdale, 1998; Campbell, 2000; Jewkes et al., 2006.
35. DeKeseredy & Olsson, 2011; DeKeseredy & Schwartz, 2009.
36. Bourgois, 1995, p. 214.
37. DeKeseredy, et al., 2007; Godenzi, Schwartz, & DeKeseredy, 2001.

38. Kimmel, 2008, pp. 225–26; emphasis in original.
39. Thornhill & Palmer, 2000.
40. Kimmel, 2008.
41. Hunnicutt, 2009.
42. Eisenstein, 1980, p. 16.
43. Ranson, 2009.
44. Faludi, 1991, p. ix.
45. DeKeseredy & Schwartz, 2003.
46. Stanko, 1997, p. 630.
47. Ferrell, Hayward, & Young, 2008; Stark, 2007; Smith, 1990; DeKeseredy & Schwartz, 1998.
48. Ellis & DeKeseredy, 1997.
49. DeKeseredy et al., 2006, p. 240.
50. DeKeseredy et al., 2006, p. 240.
51. Straus, Gelles, & Steinmetz, 1981.
52. Bancroft, 2002, p. 219.
53. Hotaling & Sugarman, 1986.

Chapter Five

1. LaViolette & Barnett, 2000, p. 10.
2. DeKeseredy & Schwartz, 2009; Sauvé & Burns, 2009; Proudfoot, 2009b.
3. Dragiewicz & DeKeseredy, 2008.
4. Denham & Gillespie, 1999.
5. Bumiller, 2008; Barker, 2009; Dragiewicz & DeKeseredy, 2008.
6. Rosen, Dragiewicz, & Gibbs, 2009.
7. DeKeseredy et al., 2003.
8. Dragiewicz & DeKeseredy, 2008. One major example of such a murder that is still widely remembered in the Durham Region is the killing of Luke Schillings. On his first unsupervised access visit in August 1997, his father strangled and burned him to death. The family court process allowed unsupervised access despite Luke's mother's pleas to allow only supervised access.
9. Horley, 1991.
10. Stark, 2007, p. 116.
11. LaViolette & Barnett, 2000, p. 11.
12. DeKeseredy & Schwartz, 1996; Conlin, Chapman, & Benson, 2006.
13. LaViolette & Barnett, 2000.
14. This section includes modified sections of work published previously by DeKeseredy & Schwartz, 1996.

15. Kirkwood, 1993.

16. Goetting, 1999; DeKeseredy & Schwartz, 2009; Bancroft, 2002; Dobash & Dobash, 1979.

17. Gosselin, 2010; Mahoney, Williams, & West, 2001; Ristock, 2002; Renzetti, 1992.

18. DeKeseredy et al., 2003; Fong, 2010; Meloy & Miller, 2011.

19. DeKeseredy & MacLeod, 1997, p. 124.

20. This section includes modified sections of work published previously by DeKeseredy & Schwartz, 1996.

21. Kirkwood, 1993, p. 73.

22. The phrase "place matters" is included in the title of Pruitt's 2008 article on violence against women in rural communities.

23. Barak, 2007, p. 89.

24. DeKeseredy et al., 2007.

25. Donnermeyer, Jobes, & Barclay, 2006, p. 199.

26. Sampson, Raudenbush, & Earls, 1998, p. 1; see also DeKeseredy et al., 2007.

27. Hay & Basran, 1992; Toughill, 2007.

28. DeKeseredy & Schwartz, 2009; Toughill, 2007; Zorza, 2002.

29. Lichter, Amundson, & Lichter, 2003; DeKeseredy & Schwartz, 2008; Brownridge, 2009.

30. DeKeseredy & Schwartz, 2009; Meloy & Miller, 2011; DeKeseredy & Schwartz, 2008; Websdale, 1998; DeKeseredy & Joseph, 2006.

31. For more information on research related to these problems, see DeKeseredy & Schwartz, 2009.

32. Cited in Hurtig, 1999, p. 88.

33. CFAFIA, 2008.

34. Ehrenreich, 2001; DeKeseredy et al., 2003.

35. CFAFIA, 2008, p. 29.

36. Davis, 1999; Stark, 2007.

37. Johnson, 1995; Meloy & Miller, 2011; DeKeseredy et al., 2003.

38. Conlin, Chapman, & Benson, 2006, pp. 36–37.

39. DeKeseredy & Schwartz, 2009, p. 88.

40. Dragiewicz & DeKeseredy, 2008.

41. DeKeseredy & Joseph, 2006, p. 303.

42. DeKeseredy et al., 2007; Lewis, 2003.

43. Wacquant, 1997, p. 346.

44. DeKeseredy & Schwartz, 2009.

45. Websdale, 1998.

46. DeKeseredy & Joseph, 2006, p. 303.

47. Dragiewicz & DeKeseredy, 2008; Conlin, Chapman, & Benson, 2006; DeKeseredy & Schwartz, 2008.

48. Goetting, 1999.

49. Ellis & DeKeseredy, 1997; Block & DeKeseredy, 2007; McFarlane & Malecha, 2005.

50. Lorena Bobbitt was an abused wife who, on June 23, 1993, cut off more than half of her husband's penis while he was sleeping in their Manassas, Virginia, apartment.

51. DeKeseredy & Schwartz, 1996, p. 326.

52. Walker, 1979.

53. Horley, 1991, p. 91.

Chapter Six

1. Sev'er, 2002, p. 188.

2. MacLeod, 1987.

3. Barnett, Miller-Perrin, & Perrin, 2005.

4. DeKeseredy & Schwartz, 2009, pp. 83–84.

5. Baker & Jaffe, 2007, p. 14.

6. Ohio Domestic Violence Network, 2008, p. 14.

7. For more information on these consequences, see National Center for Injury Prevention and Control, 2009a, 2009b; Day & McKenna 2002; and Guggisberg, 2010.

8. Dobash, Dobash, & Cavanagh, 2009.

9. Day & McKenna, 2002, p. 330.

10. Day & McKenna, 2002, pp. 342–43.

11. Barnett, Miller-Perrin, & Perrin, 2005; Day & McKenna, 2002.

12. Barnett , Miller-Perrin, & Perrin, 2005; Guggisberg, 2010.

13. DeKeseredy & Schwartz, 2009, p. 84.

14. Schwartz & DeKeseredy, 1997, p. 186.

15. Barnett, Miller-Perrin, & Perrin, 2005; Russo, 1985.

16. Grant, 2008; Guggisberg, 2010.

17. Day & McKenna, 2002, pp. 327–28.

18. National Center for Injury Prevention and Control, 2009a; Barnett, Miller-Perrin, & Perrin, 2005.

19. Ontario Government, 2007, pp. 1–2.

20. Yodanis & Godenzi, 1999.

21. DeKeseredy et al., 2006, p. 237.

22. DeKeseredy et al., 2006, p. 237.

23. Conlin, Chapman, & Benson, 2006, p. 29.

24. Johnson & Hotton, 2001.

25. Johnson & Dauvergne, 2001.

26. Baker & Jaffe, 2007.
27. Baker & Cunningham, 2005, pp. 16–17.
28. Baker & Jaffe, 2007, p. 13; see also Baker & Cunningham, 2005.
29. For the inter-generational transmission theory, see Levinson, 1989; for social learning theory, see DeKeseredy & Schwartz, 2011; for children growing up to copy their father's abuse of their mother, see Hines & Malley-Morrison, 2005.
30. Straus, Gelles, & Steinmetz, 1981, p. 122.
31. Barnett, Miller-Perrin, & Perrin, 2005; DeKeseredy & Schwartz, 2011.
32. Dobash & Dobash, 1979, p. 154.
33. Dobash & Dobash, 1979.
34. Basile et al., 2009.
35. Olweus, 1994.
36. Vallée, 2007, p. 321.
37. Eglin, 2009, p. 140.
38. Herbert, 2009.

Chapter Seven

1. Jensen, 2009, p. 88.
2. Miroslawa & Klaehn, 2009; Parenti, 2009; DeKeseredy, 2011.
3. This section includes modified parts of work published previously by Ellis & DeKeseredy, 1996; and DeKeseredy & MacLeod, 1997.
4. Peterson, 2008; DeKeseredy & Hinch, 1991; Meloy & Miller, 2011.
5. For more information on research related to this issue, see Meloy & Miller, 2011.
6. Corsianos, 2009.
7. Canadian police have always had the authority to arrest and charge wife beaters. See Meloy & Miller, 2011; DeKeseredy & Dragiewicz, 2007; Caringella, 2009.
8. Dragiewicz, 2008; Sheehy, 2002.
9. Miller, 2005, p. 133. In Canada, 70 per cent of abused women do not report assaults on them to the police; see Vallée, 2007.
10. DeKeseredy & Dragiewicz, 2007.
11. Goodmark, 2009.
12. DeKeseredy & MacLeod, 1997, p. 122.
13. Sherman & Berk, 1984. In fairness to Sherman and Berk, they point out that their data should be read with caution and that the findings may not be generalizable to all US cities.

14. Jaffe et al., 1986.
15. Peterson, 2008.
16. Dunford, Huizinga, & Elliott, 1990, p. 204.
17. DeKeseredy & Schwartz, 2009; Meloy & Miller, 2011; DeKeseredy & Dragiewicz, 2007; Bumiller, 2008; Gondolf, 2007; Miller, 2005.
18. Gondolf, 2009; DeKeseredy & Dragiewicz, 2007.
19. Currie, 1985, p. 18.
20. Renzetti, 1997, p. 262.
21. Michalowski, 1985; DeKeseredy, 2011.
22. Caringella, 2009.
23. Vallée, 2007, pp. 350–51.
24. Wilson, 1996.
25. Shepard & Pence, 1999; McMurtry, cited in Vallée, 2007, p. 341.
26. Funk, 2006.
27. Thorne-Finch, 1992, p. 236.
28. Denham & Gillespie, 1999; Jiwani, 2006; Lakeman, 2005; Rathjen & Montpetit, 1999.
29. Canadian Panel on Violence Against Women, 1993, p. 20.
30. This section includes modified sections of work published in DeKeseredy & Schwartz, 1998.
31. Caringella, 2009, p. 254.
32. DeKeseredy & Olsson, 2011.
33. Jensen, 2007, p. 182.
34. For more information on the Clean Hotel Initiative, go to www.menaspeacemakers.org/programs/mnman/hotels.
35. I am not talking here about so called "snuff" movies, where the claim is made that the woman in the movie is actually murdered. I am just talking about commonplace R- or X-rated movies that you can see on TV or on your computer screen. If the rape-murder isn't shown in graphic detail, the movie will probably be open to children. See DeKeseredy & Schwartz, 1998; Schwartz, 1987.
36. Porter, 2006, p. 1.
37. This table is adapted from one included in a pamphlet produced by the Ontario Women's Directorate, 2006, pp. 8–9.
38. Bunch, 2006, p. 1.
39. DeKeseredy, Schwartz, & Alvi, 2000.
40. Thorne-Finch, 1992; Funk, 1993.
41. Katz, 2006, p. 260.
42. This table is adapted from one included in a pamphlet produced by the Ontario Women's Directorate, 2006, p. 3.
43. Thorne-Finch, 1992, pp. 236–37; Warshaw, 1988, pp. 161–64.

44. Ontario Women's Directorate, 2006, pp. 7–8.

45. Bowker, 1998; DeKeseredy, Schwartz, & Alvi, 2000.

46. DeKeseredy & Schwartz, 2009.

47. Luxton, 1993; Sluser & Kaufman, 1992; Kilmartin, 1996; Kaufman, cited in Luxton, 1993, p. 362.

48. Thorne-Finch, 1992, p. 257.

49. DeKeseredy & MacLeod, 1997, p. 174.

50. DeKeseredy, Schwartz, & Alvi, 2000.

51. Dragiewicz, 2008; Funk, 2006.

52. Gilfus et al., 1999, p. 1207.

53. DeKeseredy, Alvi, Schwartz, & Tomaszewski, 2003; Ehrenreich, 2001.

54. Raphael, 2000, p. 125.

55. DeKeseredy, Alvi, Schwartz, & Tomaszewski, 2003.

56. DeKeseredy & Schwartz, 2002; Raphael, 2001b.

57. DeKeseredy, Alvi, Schwartz, & Tomaszewski, 2003.

58. Van Alphen, 2009.

59. Wilson, 1996; DeKeseredy, 2011.

60. Dragiewicz & DeKeseredy, 2008.

61. Aldarondo & Mederos, 2002.

62. Logan et al., 2004, p. 58.

63. DeKeseredy & Schwartz, 2009.

64. MacLeod & Shin, 1993, p. iii.

65. Malley-Morrison & Hines, 2004; DeKeseredy & MacLeod, 1997.

66. This section includes modified sections of work published by Godenzi, Schwartz, & DeKeseredy, 2001.

67. See Jensen, 2007.

68. See Katz, 2006.

69. Collins, 2000; Oliver, 2006, p. 927; Johnson, Jackson, & Gatto, 1995; Weitzer & Kubrin, 2009; Johnson, Jackson, & Gatto, 1995.

70. Barnett, Miller-Perrin, & Perrin, 2005.

71. Kutner & Olson, 2008, p. 223.

72. Bumiller, 2008.

73. United Nations, 1995, p. 95.

74. Bond & Phillips, 2001.

75. United Nations, 1993, p. 85.

76. Bond & Phillips, 2001.

77. Ledwitz-Rigby, 1993.

78. Bosworth, 2010; Reiman & Leighton, 2010; Walker, 1998.

79. Websdale, 1998; Lynch, Michalowski, & Groves, 2000.

Bibliography

Adams, A.E., Sullivan, C.M., Bybee, D., & Greeson, M.R. (2008). Development of the scale of economic abuse. *Violence Against Women*, 15, 563–88.

Adams, M., & Coltrane, S. (2005). Boys and men in families: The domestic production of gender, power, and privilege. In M.S. Kimmel, J. Hearn, & R.W. Connell (Eds.), *Handbook of studies on men & masculinities* (pp. 230–48). Thousand Oaks, CA: Sage.

Aldarondo, E., & Mederos, F. (2002). Foreword. In E. Aldarondo & F. Mederos (Eds.), *Programs for men who batter: Intervention and prevention strategies in a diverse society* (pp. ix–xi). Kingston, NJ: Civic Research Institute.

Alvarez, A., & Bachman, R. (2008). *Violence: The enduring problem*. Thousand Oaks, CA: Sage.

Alvi, S. (2009a). Visible minority women as offenders and victims. In J. Barker (Ed.), *Women and the criminal justice system: A Canadian perspective* (pp. 289–312). Toronto: Emond Montgomery.

Alvi, S. (2009b). Female youth in conflict with the law. In J. Barker (Ed.), *Women and the criminal justice system: A Canadian perspective* (pp. 229–56). Toronto: Emond Montgomery.

Anderson, K.L. (2005). Theorizing gender in intimate partner violence research. *Sex Roles*, 52, 853–65.

Angus Reid Global Monitor. (2008). Canadians reject extending Afghan mission. Retrieved January 1, 2008, from http://www.angus-reid.com/polls/view/29514.

Bibliography

AuCoin, K. (2005). *Family violence in Canada: A statistical profile 2005.* Ottawa: Statistics Canada.

Bachar, K., & Koss, M.P. (2001). From prevalence to prevention: Closing the gap between what we know about rape and what we do. In C.M. Renzetti, J.L. Edleson, & R.K. Bergen (Eds.), *Sourcebook on violence against women* (pp. 117–42). Thousand Oaks, CA: Sage.

Baker, L.L., & Cunningham, A.J. (2005). *Learning to listen, learning to help: Understanding woman abuse and its effects on children.* London, ON: Centre for Children & Families in the Justice System.

Baker, L.L., & Jaffe, P.G. (2007). *Woman abuse affects our children: An educator's guide.* Toronto: Ontario Women's Directorate.

Bancroft, L. (2002). *Why does he do that? Inside the minds of angry and controlling men.* New York: Penguin.

Barak, G. (2007). *Violence, conflict, and world order: Critical conversations on state-sanctioned justice.* Lanham, MD: Rowman & Littlefield.

Barker, J. (2009). Background experiences of women offenders. In J. Barker (Ed.), *Women and the criminal justice system: A Canadian perspective* (pp. 89–114). Toronto: Emond Montgomery.

Barnett, O.W., Miller-Perrin, C.L., & Perrin, R.D. (2005). *Family violence across the lifespan: An introduction,* 2nd ed. Thousand Oaks, CA: Sage.

Basile, K.C., Espelage, D.L., Rivers, I., McMahon, P.M., & Simon, T.R. (2009). The theoretical and empirical links between bullying behavior and male sexual violence perpetration. *Aggression and Violent Behavior,* 14, 337–47.

Becker, H.S. (1973). *Outsiders; Studies in the sociology of deviance.* New York: Free Press.

Bell, C.C., & Matis, J. (2000). The importance of cultural competence in ministering to African American victims of domestic violence. *Violence Against Women,* 6, 515–32.

Benson, M.L., & Fox, G.L. (2004). *When violence hits home: How economics and neighborhoods play a role.* Washington, DC: US Department of Justice.

Bergen, R.K. (1996). *Wife rape: Understanding the response of survivors and service providers.* Thousand Oaks, CA: Sage.

Bergen, R.K., & Bogle, K.A. (2000). Exploring the connection between pornography and sexual violence. *Violence and Victims,* 15, 227–34.

Betowski, B. (2007). 1 in 3 boys heavy porn users, study shows. Retrieved February 23, 2007, from http://www.eurekalert.org/pub_releases/2007-02/uoa-oit022307.php.

Block, C.R. (2000). *The Chicago women's health risk study*. Washington, DC: US Department of Justice.

Block, C.R., & DeKeseredy, W.S. (2007). Forced sex and leaving intimate relationships: Results of the Chicago women's health risk study. *Women's Health and Urban Life*, 6, 6–23.

Bograd, M. (1988). Feminist perspectives on wife abuse: An introduction. In K. Yllo & M. Bograd (Eds.), *Feminist perspectives on wife abuse* (pp. 11–26). Newbury Park, CA: Sage.

Bond, J., & Phillips, R. (2001). Violence against women as a human rights violation: International institutional responses. In C.M. Renzetti, J.L. Edleson, & R.K. Bergen (Eds.), *Sourcebook on violence against women* (pp. 481–500). Thousand Oaks, CA: Sage.

Bonisteel, M., & Green, L. (2005). Implications of the shrinking space for feminist anti-violence advocacy. Retrieved February 6, 2009, from http://www.crvawc.ca/documents/ShrinkingFeministSpace_AntiViolenceAdvocacy_OCT2005.pdf.

Bosworth, M. (2010). *Explaining US imprisonment*. Thousand Oaks, CA: Sage.

Bourgois, P. (1995). *In search of respect: Selling crack in El Barrio*. New York: Cambridge University Press.

Bowker, L.H. (1983). *Beating wife-beating*. Lexington, MA: Lexington Books.

Bowker, L.H. (1998). On the difficulty of eradicating masculine violence: Multisystem overdetermination. In L.H. Bowker (Ed.), *Masculinities and violence* (pp. 1–14). Thousand Oaks, CA: Sage.

Brownridge, D.A., (2009). *Violence against women: Vulnerable populations*. New York: Routledge.

Brownridge, D.A., & Halli, S.S. (2001). *Explaining violence against women in Canada*. Lanham, MD: Lexington Books.

Brzozowski, J., Taylor-Butts, A., & Johnson, S. (2006). *Victimization and offending among the Aboriginal population in Canada*. Ottawa: Statistics Canada.

Bumiller, K. (2008). *In an abusive state: How neoliberalism appropriated the feminist movement against sexual violence*. Durham, NC: Duke University Press.

Bunch, T. (2006). *Ending men's violence against women*. New York: A Call to Men, National Association of Men and Women Committed to Ending Violence Against Women.

Cameron, S. (2007). *The Pickton file*. Toronto: Knopf Canada.

Campbell, H. (2000). The glass phallus: Pub(lic) masculinity and drinking in rural New Zealand. *Rural Sociology*, 65, 562–81.

Bibliography

Canadian Feminist Alliance for International Action (CFAFIA).
(2008). *Women's inequality in Canada*. Ottawa: Statistics Canada.

CanadianLawSite.Com. (2004). Canadian family violence laws.
Retrieved August 12, 2004, from http://www.canadianlawsite.com/
family-violence-laws.htm.

Canadian Panel on Violence Against Women. (1993). *Changing the
landscape: Ending violence—achieving equality*. Ottawa: Ministry of
Supply and Services Canada.

Carastathis, A. (2006). New cuts and conditions for Status of Women
Canada. *Toronto Star*, October 11. Retrieved October 11, 2006, from
www.dominionpaper.ca/canadian_news/2006/10/11new_cuts_a.html.

Caringella, S. (2009). *Addressing rape reform in law and practice*. New
York: Columbia University Press.

CBC News. (2010). Retrieved August 12, 2010 from http://www.cbc.
ca/news/background/afghanistan/casualties/list.html.

Chesney-Lind, M. (1999). Review of Patricia Pearson's *When she was
bad: Violent women and the myth of innocence*. *Women & Criminal
Justice*, 10, 114–18.

Chesney-Lind, M., & Eliason, M. (2006). From invisible to
incorrigible: The demonization of marginalized women and girls.
Crime, Media, and Culture, 2, 29–47.

Chesney-Lind, M., & Irwin, K. (2008). *Beyond bad girls: Gender,
violence, and hype*. New York: Routledge.

Christensen, F. (2002). Prostituted science and scholarship: A
submission to the Special Senate-Commons Committee on
Custody and Access. Retrieved July 3, 2002, from http://www.
fathers.bc.ca/prostituted_science.htm.

Cobb, C. (1998). Divorce panel "taunts" women: Women who report
abuse are intimidated, MP charges. *Ottawa Citizen*, June 15, A3.

Cohen, S. (1980). *Folk devils and moral panics*. Oxford: Basil Blackwell.

Collins, P.H. (2000). *Black feminist thought*, 2nd ed. New York:
Routledge.

Comack, E. (1993). Feminist engagement with the law: The legal
recognition of the battered woman syndrome. *The CRIAW Papers*.
Ottawa: Canadian Research Institute for the Advancement of
Women.

Conlin, T., Chapman, J., & Benson, R. (2006). *After she leaves: A
training & resource manual for volunteers and staff supporting
woman abuse survivors & their children during the family law process*.
Toronto: Ministry of the Attorney General.

Connell, R.W. (1995). *Masculinities*. Berkeley: University of California
Press.

Contenta, S., Rankin, J., Powell, B., & Winsa, P. (2008). Why getting tough on crime is toughest on the taxpayer. *Toronto Star*, July 19, A1, A14–A15.

Corry, J. (1801). *A satirical view of London at the commencement of the nineteenth century*. London: G. Kearsley.

Corsianos, M. (2009). *Policing and gendered justice: Examining the possibilities*. Toronto: University of Toronto Press.

Cross, P. (2007). Femicide: Violent partners create war zone for women. *Toronto Star*, July 6, A8.

Currie, E. (1985). *Confronting crime: An American challenge*. New York: Pantheon.

Currie, E. (2004). *The road to whatever: Middle-class culture and the crisis of adolescence*. New York: Metropolitan Books.

Dasgupta, S.D. (2002). A framework for understanding women's use of nonlethal violence in intimate relationships. *Violence Against Women*, 8, 1364–89.

Dauvergne, M., & Li, G. (2006). *Homicide in Canada, 2005*. Ottawa: Canadian Centre for Justice Statistics, Statistics Canada.

Davis, M.F. (1999). The economics of abuse: How violence perpetuates women's poverty. In R.A. Brandwein (Ed.), *Battered women, children, and welfare reform: The ties that bind* (pp. 17–30). Thousand Oaks, CA: Sage.

Day, T., & McKenna, K.M.J. (2002). The health-related economic costs of violence against women in Canada: The tip of the iceberg. In M.J. McKenna & J. Larkin (Eds.), *Violence against women: New Canadian perspectives* (pp. 313–50). Toronto: Inanna.

DeKeseredy, W.S. (1990). Male peer support and woman abuse: The current state of knowledge. *Sociological Focus*, 23, 129–39.

DeKeseredy, W.S. (2000). Current controversies in defining nonlethal violence against women in intimate heterosexual relationships: Empirical implications. *Violence Against Women*, 6, 728–46.

DeKeseredy, W.S. (2006). Future directions. *Violence against women*, 12, 1078–85.

DeKeseredy, W.S. (2007). Factoids that challenge efforts to curb violence against women. *Domestic Violence Report*, 12, 81–82, 93–95.

DeKeseredy, W.S. (2009a). Patterns of violence in the family. In M. Baker (Ed.), *Families: Changing trends in Canada* (pp. 179–205). Whitby, ON: McGraw-Hill Ryerson.

DeKeseredy, W.S. (2009b). Girls and women as victims of crime. In J. Barker (Ed.), *Women and the criminal justice system: A Canadian perspective* (pp. 313–45). Toronto: Emond Montgomery.

DeKeseredy, W.S. (2009c). Canadian crime control in the new millennium: The influence of neo-conservative policies and practices. *Police Practice and Research*, 10, 305–16.

DeKeseredy, W.S. (2009d). Male violence against women in North America as hate crime. In B. Perry (Ed.), *Hate crimes*, Vol. 3: *The victims of hate crime* (pp. 151–72). Santa Barbara, CA: Praeger.

DeKeseredy, W.S. (2010). Epilogue: Moral panics, violence, and the policing of girls: Reasserting patriarchal control in the new millennium. In M. Chesney-Lind & N. Jones (Eds.), *Fighting for girls: New perspectives on gender and violence*. Albany: SUNY Press.

DeKeseredy, W.S. (2011). *Contemporary critical criminology*. London: Routledge.

DeKeseredy, W.S., Alvi, S., & Schwartz, M.D. (2006). An economic exclusion/male peer support model looks at "wedfare" and woman abuse. *Critical Criminology*, 14, 23–41.

DeKeseredy, W.S., Alvi, S., Schwartz, M.D., & Tomaszewski, E.A. (2003). *Under siege: Poverty and crime in a public housing community*. Lanham, MD: Lexington Books.

DeKeseredy, W.S., Donnermeyer, J.F., Schwartz, M.D., Tunnell, K.D., & Hall, M. (2007). Thinking critically about rural gender relations: Toward a rural masculinity crisis/male peer support model of separation/divorce sexual assault. *Critical Criminology*, 15, 295–311.

DeKeseredy, W.S., & Dragiewicz, M. (2007). Understanding the complexities of feminist perspectives on woman abuse: A commentary on Donald G. Dutton's *Rethinking domestic violence*. *Violence Against Women*, 13, 874–84.

DeKeseredy, W.S., & Dragiewicz, M. (2009). *Shifting public policy direction: Gender-focused versus bidirectional intimate partner violence*. Report prepared for the Ontario Women's Directorate. Toronto: Ontario Women's Directorate.

DeKeseredy, W.S., Ellis, D., & Alvi, S. (2005). *Deviance and crime: Theory, research, and policy*. Cincinnati: LexisNexis.

DeKeseredy, W.S., & Flack, W.F. (2007). Sexual assault in colleges and universities. In G. Barak (Ed.), *Battleground criminal justice* (pp. 693–97). Westport, CT: Greenwood.

DeKeseredy, W.S., & Hinch, R. (1991). *Woman abuse: Sociological perspectives*. Toronto: Thompson Educational Publishing.

DeKeseredy, W.S., & Joseph, C. (2006). Separation/divorce sexual assault in rural Ohio: Preliminary results of an exploratory study. *Violence Against Women*, 12, 301–11.

DeKeseredy, W.S., & MacLeod, L. (1997). *Woman abuse: A sociological story*. Toronto: Harcourt Brace.

DeKeseredy, W.S., & Olsson, P. (2011). Adult pornography, male peer support, and violence against women: The contribution of the "dark side" of the Internet. In M. Varga Martin, M.A. Garcia-Ruiz, & A. Edwards (Eds.), *Technology for facilitating humanity and combating social deviations: Interdisciplinary perspectives* (pp. 34–50). Hershey, PA: IGI Global.

DeKeseredy, W.S., Perry, B., & Schwartz, M.D. (2007). Hate-motivated sexual assault on the college campus: Results from a Canadian representative sample. Paper presented at the annual meetings of the American Society of Criminology, Atlanta.

DeKeseredy, W.S., Rogness, M., & Schwartz, M.D. (2004). Separation/divorce sexual assault: The current state of social scientific knowledge. *Aggression and Violent Behavior, 9*, 675–91.

DeKeseredy, W.S., & Schwartz, M.D. (1996). *Contemporary criminology*. Belmont, CA: Wadsworth.

DeKeseredy, W.S., & Schwartz, M.D. (1998). *Woman abuse on campus: Results from the Canadian national survey*. Thousand Oaks, CA: Sage.

DeKeseredy, W.S., & Schwartz, M.D. (2001). Definitional issues. In C.M. Renzetti, J.L. Edleson, & R.K. Bergen (Eds.), *Sourcebook on violence against women* (pp. 23–34). Thousand Oaks, CA: Sage.

DeKeseredy, W.S., & Schwartz, M.D. (2002). Theorizing public housing woman abuse as a function of economic exclusion and male peer support. *Women's Health and Urban Life, 1*, 26–45.

DeKeseredy, W.S., & Schwartz, M.D. (2003). Backlash and whiplash: A critique of Statistics Canada's 1999 General Social Survey on Victimization. Retrieved July 13, 2010, from http://sisyphe.org/article.php3?id_article=1689.

DeKeseredy, W.S., & Schwartz, M.D. (2008). Separation/divorce sexual assault in rural Ohio: Survivors' perceptions. *Journal of Prevention & Intervention in the Community, 36*, 105–20.

DeKeseredy, W.S., & Schwartz, M.D. (2009). *Dangerous exits: Escaping abusive relationships in rural America*. New Brunswick, NJ: Rutgers University Press.

DeKeseredy, W.S., & Schwartz, M.D. (2011). Theoretical and definitional issues in violence against women. In C.M. Renzetti, J.L. Edleson, & R.K. Bergen (Eds.), *Sourcebook on violence against women*, 2nd ed. (pp. 3–22). Thousand Oaks, CA: Sage.

Bibliography

DeKeseredy, W.S., Schwartz, M.D., & Alvi, S. (2000). The role of profeminist men in dealing with woman abuse on the Canadian college campus. *Violence Against Women*, 9, 918–35.

DeKeseredy, W.S., Schwartz, M.D., Fagen, D., & Hall, M. (2006). Separation/divorce sexual assault: The contribution of male peer support. *Feminist Criminology*, 1, 228–50.

Denham, D., & Gillespie, J. (1999). *Two steps forward...one step back: An overview of Canadian initiatives and resources to end woman abuse 1989–1997*. Ottawa: Health Canada.

Desai, S., & Saltzman, L.E. (2001). Measurement issues for violence against women. In C.M. Renzetti, J.L. Edleson, & R.K. Bergen (Eds.), *Sourcebook on violence against women* (pp. 35–52). Thousand Oaks, CA: Sage.

Dobash, R.E., & Dobash, R.P. (1979). *Violence against wives: A case against the patriarchy*. New York: Free Press.

Dobash, R.E., & Dobash, R.P. (1992). *Women, violence, & social change*. London: Routledge.

Dobash, R.E., Dobash, R.P., & Cavanagh, K. (2009). Out of the blue: Men who murder an intimate partner. *Feminist Criminology*, 4, 194–225.

Dobash, R.P., Dobash, R.E., Wilson, M., & Daly, M. (1992). The myth of sexual symmetry in marital violence. *Social Problems*, 39, 71–91.

Domestic Violence Death Review Committee. (2004). *Annual report to the Chief Coroner: 2004*. Toronto: Office of the Chief Coroner of Ontario.

Domestic Violence Death Review Committee. (2005). *Annual report to the Chief Coroner: 2005*. Toronto: Office of the Chief Coroner of Ontario.

Domestic Violence Death Review Committee. (2007). *Fifth annual report of the Domestic Violence Death Review Committee*. Toronto: Office of the Chief Coroner of Ontario.

Donnermeyer, J.F., Jobes, P., & Barclay, E. (2006). Rural crime, poverty, and community. In W.S. DeKeseredy & B. Perry (Eds.), *Advancing critical criminology: Theory and application* (pp. 199–218). Lanham, MD: Lexington Books.

Dragiewicz, M. (2008). Patriarchy reasserted: Fathers' rights and anti-VAWA activism. *Feminist Criminology*, 3, 121–44.

Dragiewicz, M. (2009). Why sex and gender matter in domestic violence research and advocacy. In E. Stark & E.S. Buzawa (Eds.), *Violence against women in families and relationships*, Vol. 3: *Criminal justice and law* (pp. 201–15). Santa Barbara, CA: Praeger.

Dragiewicz, M., & DeKeseredy, W.S. (2008). *A needs gap assessment report on abused women without legal representation in the family courts*. Oshawa, ON: Report prepared for Luke's Place Support and Resource Centre.

Duffy, A., & Momirov, J. (1997). *Family violence: A Canadian introduction*. Toronto: Lorimer.

Dunford, F., Huizinga, D., & Elliott, D.S. (1990). The role of arrest in domestic assault: The Omaha police experiment. *Criminology*, 28, 183–206.

Dutton, D.G. (2006). *Rethinking domestic violence*. Vancouver: University of British Columbia Press.

Edin, K. (2000). What do low-income single mothers say about marriage? *Social Problems*, 47, 112–33.

Edwards, P. (2009). Huge porn bust frees 2 children. *Toronto Star*, February 6, A3.

Eglin, P. (2009). Marc Lépine and me: What I learned from the Montreal massacre. In J. Klaehn (Ed.), *Roadblocks to equality: Women challenging boundaries* (pp. 133–54). Montreal: Black Rose Books.

Ehrenreich, B. (2001). *Nickel and dimed: On (not) getting by in America*. New York: Metropolitan Books.

Eisenstein, Z. (1980). *Capitalist patriarchy and the case for socialist feminism*. New York: Monthly Review Press.

Elias, R. (1986). *The politics of victimization: Victimology and human rights*. New York: Oxford University Press.

Elizabeth Fry Society. (2009). *Aboriginal women, 2009*. Retrieved March 8, 2010, from http://www.elizabethfry.ca/eweek06/pdf/aborig.pdf.

Ellis, D. (1987). *The wrong stuff: An introduction to the sociological study of deviance*. Toronto: Collier Macmillan.

Ellis, D., & DeKeseredy, W.S. (1996). *The wrong stuff: An introduction to the sociological study of deviance*, 2nd ed. Toronto: Allyn & Bacon.

Ellis, D., & DeKeseredy, W.S. (1997). Rethinking estrangement, interventions, and intimate femicide. *Violence Against Women*, 3, 590–609.

Fagen, D. (2005). *Perceptions of collective efficacy among abused women in rural Appalachia*. M.A. Thesis, Department of Sociology and Anthropology, Ohio University.

Faith, K. (1993). *Unruly women: The politics of confinement and resistance*. Vancouver: Press Gang.

Faludi, S. (1991). *Backlash: The undeclared war against American women*. New York: Crown.

Bibliography

Farrell, J. (2002). Brochure spread anti-male bias: Panel. *Calgary Herald*. Retrieved June 19, 2002, from http://www.mesacanada.com/brochure.htm.

Fekete, J. (1994). *Moral panic: Biopolitics rising*. Montreal: Robert Davies.

Ferrell, J., Hayward, K., & Young, J. (2008). *Cultural criminology: An invitation*. London: Sage.

Fitzpatrick, D., & Halliday, C. (1992). *Not the way to love*. Amherst, NS: Cumberland County Transition House Association.

Follingstad, D.R., Rutledge, L.L., Berg, B.J., Hause, E.S., & Polek, D.S. (1990). The role of emotional abuse in physically abusive relationships. *Journal of Family Violence*, 5, 107–20.

Fong, J. (2010). Introduction. In J. Fong (Ed.), *Out of the shadows: Woman abuse in ethnic, immigrant, and Aboriginal communities* (pp. 2–6). Toronto: Women's Press.

Fox, B.J. (1993). On violent men and female victims: A comment on DeKeseredy and Kelly. *Canadian Journal of Sociology*, 18, 320–24.

Funk, R.E. (1993). *Stopping rape: A challenge for men*. Philadelphia: New Society Publishers.

Funk, R.E. (2006). *Reaching men: Strategies for preventing sexist attitudes, behaviors, and violence*. Indianapolis: JIST Life.

Garbarino, J. (2006). *See Jane hit: Why girls are growing more violent and what we can do about it*. New York: Penguin Press.

Garcia-Moreno, C., Jansen, A.F.M.H., Ellsberg, M., Heise, L., & Watts, C. (2005). *WHO multi-country study on women's health and domestic violence against women: Initial results on prevalence, health outcomes, and women's responses*. Geneva: World Health Organization.

Gartner, R., Dawson, M., & Crawford, M. (2001). Women killing: Intimate femicide in Ontario, 1874–1994. In D.E.H. Russell & R.A. Harmes (Eds.), *Femicide in global perspective* (pp. 147–65). New York: Teachers College Press.

Gayford, J.J. (1975). Wife battering: A preliminary survey of 100 cases. *British Medical Journal*, 1, 194–97.

Gelles, R.J., & Cavanaugh, M.M. (2005). Association is not causation: Alcohol and other drugs do not cause violence. In D.R. Loseke, R.J. Gelles, & M.M. Cavanaugh (Eds.), *Current controversies on family violence*, 2nd ed. (pp. 175–89). Thousand Oaks, CA: Sage.

Gelles, R.J., & Straus, M.A. (1988). *Intimate violence: The causes and consequences of abuse in the American family*. New York: Simon & Schuster.

Gilfus, M.E., Fineran, S., Cohan, D.J., Jensen, S.A., Hartwick, L., & Spath, R. (1999). Research on violence against women: Creating survivor-informed collaborations. *Violence Against Women*, 5, 1194–1212.

Gillespie, I. (2008). Nowadays, it's brutal, accessible; pornography. *London Free Press*, June 11, A3.

Glassner, B. (1999). *The culture of fear*. New York: Basic Books.

Goar, G. (2009). The sad fate of too many native women. *Toronto Star*, May 20, A23.

Goddard, J. (2009). Study links childhood abuse to increased risk of cancer. *Toronto Star*, June 26, A2.

Godenzi, A., Schwartz, M.D., & DeKeseredy, W.S. (2001). Toward a gendered social bond/male peer support theory of university woman abuse. *Critical Criminology*, 10, 1–16.

Goetting, A. (1999). *Getting out: Life stories of women who left abusive men*. New York: Columbia University Press.

Gondolf, E.W. (1999). MCMI results for batterer program participants in four cities: Less "pathological" than expected. *Journal of Family Violence*, 14, 1–17.

Gondolf, E.W. (2007). Unpublished letter to the *New York Times*, August 8.

Gondolf, E.W. (2009). Personal communication, May 27.

Goodmark, L. (2008). When is a battered woman not a battered woman? When she fights back. *Yale Journal of Law and Feminism*, 20, 76–129.

Goodmark, L. (2009). Autonomy feminism: An anti-essentialist critique of mandatory interventions in domestic violence cases. *Florida State University Law Review*. Retrieved December 18, 2009, from http://ssn.com.

Gosselin, D.K. (2010). *Heavy hands: An introduction to the crimes of family violence*. Boston: Prentice Hall.

Grabb, E., & Curtis, J. (2005). *Regions apart: The four societies of Canada and the United States*. Toronto: Oxford University Press.

Grant, J. (2008). *Charting women's journeys: From addiction to recovery*. Lanham, MD: Lexington.

Guggisberg, M. (2010). *An exploratory study of the relationship between female intimate partner violence, victimization, mental health problems, and substance use issues.* Doctoral dissertation, School of Population Health & Law School, University of Western Australia.

Gumus, G. (2006). Alcohol consumption and unemployment. Paper presented at the annual meeting of the Economics of Population Health: Inaugural Conference of the American Society of Health Economists, Madison, WI.

Hall, R. (1985). *Ask any woman: A London inquiry into rape and sexual assault*. London: Falling Wall Press.

Hall, S. (1999). Reena Virk: A disposable kid to cruel attackers. *Vancouver Sun*, May 8, A10.

Hammer, R. (2002). *Antifeminism and family terrorism: A critical feminist perspective*. Lanham, MD: Rowman & Littlefield.

Hatt, K., Caputo, T.C., & Perry, B. (1990). Managing consent: Canada's experience with neo-conservatism. *Social Justice*, 17, 30–48.

Hay, D., & Basran, G.S. (1992). Introduction. In D.A. Hay & G.S. Basran (Eds.), *Rural sociology in Canada* (pp. ix–x). Toronto: Oxford University Press.

Henry, M., & Powell, B. (2007). Double tragedy turns joy to grief: Husband charged as woman expecting first child in December is slain; efforts to save fetus fail. *Toronto Star*, October 3, A1, A10.

Herbert, B. (2009). Women at risk. *New York Times*. Retrieved August 8, 2009, from http://www.nytimes.com/2009/08/08/opinion/08herbert.html?_r=1&.

Hickey, E. (2005). *Serial Murderers and their victims.* Belmont, CA: Wadsworth.

Hines, D., & Malley-Morrison, K. (2005). *Family violence in the United States: Defining, understanding, and combating abuse*. Thousand Oaks, CA: Sage.

Horley, S. (1991). *The charm syndrome: Why charming men can make dangerous lovers*. London: Papermac.

Hotaling, G., & Sugarman, D. (1986). An analysis of risk markers and husband to wife violence: The current state of knowledge. *Violence and Victims*, 1, 102–24.

Hunnicutt, G. (2009). Varieties of patriarchy and violence against women: Resurrecting "patriarchy" as a theoretical tool. *Violence Against Women*, 15, 553–73.

Hurtig, M. (1999). *Pay the rent or feed the kids: The tragedy and disgrace of poverty in Canada*. Toronto: McClelland & Stewart.

Independent Women's Forum. (2002). Nancy M. Pfotenhauer, Margot Hill appointed to the VAWA Advisory Committee. Retrieved March 10, 2007, from http//www.iwf.org/media/media_list.asp?page=1&fType=37.

Jaffe, P., Wolfe, D., Telford, A., & Austin, G. (1986). The impact of police charges in incidents of wife abuse. *Journal of Family Violence*, 1, 37–49.

Jasinski, J.L., Wesely, J.K., Wright, J.D., & Mustaine, E.E. (2010). *Hard lives, mean streets: Violence in the lives of homeless women*. Boston: Northeastern University Press.

Jensen, R. (2007). *Getting off: Pornography and the end of masculinity*. Cambridge, MA: South End Press.

Jensen, R. (2009). Just prudes? Feminism, pornography, and men's responsibility. In J. Klaehn (Ed.), *Roadblocks to equality: Women challenging boundaries* (pp. 88–100). Montreal: Black Rose Books.

Jewkes, R., Dunkle, K., Koss, M.P., Levin, J.B., Nduna, M., Jama, N., & Sikweyiya, Y. (2006). Rape perpetration by young rural South African men: Prevalence, patterns, and risk factors. *Social Science and Medicine*, 63, 2949–2961.

Jiwani, J. (2000). The 1999 General Social Survey on spousal violence: An analysis. Retrieved July 3, 2001, from http://www.casac.ca/survey99.htm.

Jiwani, J. (2006). *Discourses of denial: Mediations of race, gender, and violence*. Vancouver: University of British Columbia Press.

Johnson, A.G. (1997). *The gender knot: Unraveling our patriarchal legacy*. Philadelphia: Temple University Press.

Johnson, H. (1996). *Dangerous domains: Violence against women in Canada*. Scarborough, ON: Nelson Canada.

Johnson, H. (2006). *Measuring violence against women: Statistical trends*. Ottawa: Statistics Canada.

Johnson, H., & Dauvergne, M. (2001). *Children witnessing family violence, 1999–2000*. Ottawa: Canadian Centre for Justice Statistics.

Johnson, H., & Hotton, T. (2001). Spousal violence. In C. Trainor & K. Mihorean (Eds.), *Family violence in Canada: A statistical profile 2001*. Ottawa: Statistics Canada.

Johnson, H., Ollus, N., & Nevala, S. (2008). *Violence against women: An international perspective*. New York: Springer.

Johnson, H., & Sacco, V.F. (1995). Researching violence against women: Statistics Canada's national survey. *Canadian Journal of Criminology*, 37, 281–304.

Johnson, J.D., Jackson, L.A., & Gatto, L. (1995). Violent attitudes and deferred academic aspirations: Deleterious effects of exposure to rap music. *Basic and Applied Social Psychology*, 16, 27–41.

Johnson, M.P. (1995). Patriarchal violence and common couple violence: Two forms of violence against women. *Journal of Marriage and the Family*, 57, 283–94.

Johnson, M.P. (2008). *A typology of domestic violence: Intimate terrorism, violent resistance, and situational couple violence*. Boston: Northeastern University Press.

Bibliography

Jones, T., & Newburn, T. (2002). Learning from Uncle Sam? Exploring US influences on British crime control policy. *Governance*, 15, 97–119.

Katz, J. (2006). *The macho paradox: Why some men hurt women and how all men can help*. Naperville, IL: Sourcebooks.

Kelly, K. (1994). The politics of data. *Canadian Journal of Sociology*, 19, 81–85.

Kernsmith, P. (2008). Coercive control. In C.M. Renzetti & J.L. Edleson (Eds.), *Encyclopedia of interpersonal violence* (pp. 133–34). Thousand Oaks, CA: Sage.

Kettani, A. (2009). Out from the shadows: Women's studies programs have changed how we view violence against women. *University Affairs*, June-July, 19.

Kilmartin, C.T. (1996). The White Ribbon Campaign: Men working to end men's violence against women. *Journal of College Student Development*, May/June, 347–48.

Kilpatrick, D.G. (2004). What is violence against women? Defining and measuring the problem. *Journal of Interpersonal Violence*, 19, 1209–1234.

Kimmel, M. (2008). *Guyland: The perilous world where boys become men*. New York: Harper.

Kirkwood, C. (1993). *Leaving abusive partners*. Newbury Park, CA: Sage.

Kome, P.J. (2009). Amazon declines to sell "Rapelay" video game. Retrieved February 16, 2009, from http://www.telegraph.co.uk/scienceandtechnology/technology/4611161/rapelay-virtual-rape-game-banned-by-Amazon.html.

Kowalski, M. (2006). Spousal homicides. In L. Ogrodnik (Ed.), *Family violence in Canada: A statistical profile* (pp. 52–57). Ottawa: Statistics Canada.

Krug, E., Dahlberg, E.L., Mercy, J., Zwi, A.B., & Lozano, R. (2002). *World report on violence and health*. Geneva: World Health Organization.

Kutner, L., & Olson, C.K. (2008). *Grand theft childhood: The surprising truth about violent video games*. New York: Simon & Schuster.

Lakeman, L. (2005). *Obsession with intent: Violence against women*. Montreal: Black Rose Books.

LaViolette, A.D., & Barnett, O.W. (2000). *It could happen to anyone: Why battered women stay*. Thousand Oaks, CA: Sage.

Ledwitz-Rigby, F. (1993). An administrative approach to personal safety on campus: The role of a president's advisory committee on women's safety on campus. *Journal of Human Justice*, 4, 85–94.

Levinson, D. (1989). *Family violence in cross-cultural perspective.*
Newbury Park, CA: Sage.

Lewis, S.H. (2003). *Unspoken crimes: Sexual assault in rural America.*
Enola, PA: National Sexual Violence Resource Center.

Lichter, S.R., Amundson, D., & Lichter, L.S. (2003). *Perceptions of rural America: Media coverage.* Washington, DC: W.K. Kellogg Foundation.

Logan, T.K., Stevenson, E., Evans, L., & Leukefeld, C. (2004). Rural and urban women's perceptions of barriers to health, mental health, and criminal justice services: Implications for victim services. *Violence and Victims,* 19, 37–62.

Lombroso, C., & Ferrero, W. (1895). *The female offender.* New York: Philosophical Library.

Luxton, M. (1993). Dreams and dilemmas: Feminist musings on "the man question." In T. Haddad (Ed.), *Men and masculinities* (pp. 347–74). Toronto: Canadian Scholars' Press.

Lynch, M.J., Michalowski, R., & Groves, W.B. (2000). *The new primer in radical criminology: Critical perspectives on crime, power and identity,* 3rd ed. Monsey, NJ: Criminal Justice Press.

MacLeod, L. (1987). *Battered but not beaten: Preventing wife battering in Canada.* Ottawa: Canadian Advisory Council on the Status of Women.

MacLeod, L., & Shin, M. (1993). *Like a wingless bird: A tribute to the survival and courage of women who are abused and who speak neither English nor French.* Ottawa: Department of Canadian Heritage.

Mahoney, P., Williams, L., & West, C.M. (2001). Violence against women by intimate relationship partners. In C.M. Renzetti, J.L. Edleson, & R.K. Bergen (Eds.), *Sourcebook on violence against women* (pp. 143–78). Thousand Oaks, CA: Sage.

Males, M. (2010). Have "girls gone wild?" In M. Chesney-Lind & N. Jones (Eds.), *Fighting for girls: New perspectives on gender and violence.* Albany: SUNY Press.

Malley-Morrison, K., & Hines, D.A. (2004). *Family violence in a cultural perspective: Defining, understanding, and combating abuse.* Thousand Oaks, CA: Sage.

McFarlane, J., & Malecha, A. (2005). *Sexual assault among intimates: Frequency, consequences, and treatments.* Washington, DC: Department of Justice, National Institute of Justice.

Meloy, M.L., & Miller, S.L. (2011). *The victimization of women.* New York: Oxford University Press.

Menard, A. (2001). Domestic violence and housing: Key policy and program challenges. *Violence Against Women,* 7, 707–21.

Bibliography

Michalowski, R.J. (1985). *Order, law, and crime: An introduction to criminology*. New York: Random House.

Mihalic, S.W., & Elliot, D. (1997). If violence is domestic, does it really count? *Journal of Family Violence*, 12, 293–311.

Mihorean, K. (2005). Trends in self-reported spousal violence. In K. AuCoin (Ed.), *Family violence in Canada: A statistical profile 2005* (pp. 13–32). Ottawa: Statistics Canada.

Miller, J. (2008). *Getting played: African American girls, urban inequality, and gendered violence*. New York: New York University Press.

Miller, S.L. (2005). *Victims as offenders: The paradox of women's violence in relationships*. New Brunswick, NJ: Rutgers University Press.

Mills, C.W. (1956). *The power elite*. New York: Oxford University Press.

Mills, C.W. (1959). *The sociological imagination*. New York: Oxford University Press.

Miroslawa, A., & Klaehn, J. (2009). An introduction. In J. Klaehn (Ed.), *Roadblocks to equality: Women challenging boundaries* (p.103). Montreal: Black Rose Books.

Muehlenhard, C.L., Powch, I.G., Phelps, J.L., & Giusti, L.M. (1992). Definitions of rape: Scientific and political implications. *Journal of Social Issues*, 48, 23–44.

Mujica, A., & Ayala, A.I.U. (2008). Femicide in Morelos: An issue on public health. Paper presented at the World Health Organization's 9th World Conference on Injury Prevention and Safety Promotion, Yucatan, Mexico.

National Center for Injury Prevention and Control. (2009a). *Sexual violence and intimate partner violence*. Atlanta: Centers for Disease Control and Prevention.

National Center for Injury Prevention and Control. (2009b). *Uniform definitions for sexual violence.* Atlanta: Centers for Disease Control and Prevention.

National Institute of Justice. (2000). Workshop on gender symmetry. Retrieved March 2, 2008, from http://www.ojp.usdoj.gov/nij/topics/crime/violence-against-women/workshops/gender-symmetry.htm.

Native Women's Association of Canada. (2008). *Aboriginal women in the Canadian criminal justice system*. Oshweken, ON: Native Women's Association of Canada.

Ogrodnik, L. (2008). Spousal homicides. In L. Ogrodnik (Ed.), *Family violence in Canada: A statistical profile 2008* (p. 39). Ottawa: Statistics Canada.

Ohio Domestic Violence Network. (2008). *Increasing safety for Ohio families*. Columbus: Ohio Domestic Violence Network.

Oliver, W. (2006). The streets: An alternative black male socialization institution. *Journal of Black Studies*, 36, 918–37.

Olsson, P. (2003). *Legal ideals and normative realities: A case study of children's rights and child labor activity in Paraguay*. Lund, Sweden: Lund University.

Olweus, D. (1994). Bullying at school: Long-term outcomes for the victims and an effective school-based intervention program. In L.R. Huesmann (Ed.), *Aggressive behavior: Current perspectives* (pp. 97–130). New York: Plenum Press.

Ontario Government. (2007). *Domestic violence action plan: Update— January 2007*. Toronto: Ontario Government.

Ontario Women's Directorate. (2006). *Neighbours, friends, and families: How to talk to men who are abusive*. Toronto: Government of Ontario.

Parenti, M. (2009). Custom against women. In J. Klaehn (Ed.), *Roadblocks to equality: Women challenging boundaries* (pp. 129–32). Montreal: Black Rose Books.

Pearson, L., & Gallaway, R. (1998). *For the sake of the children: Report of the Special Joint Committee on Child Custody and Access*. Ottawa: Public Works and Government Services Canada.

Pearson, P. (1997). *When she was bad: Violent women and the myth of innocence*. Toronto: Random House Canada.

Pence, E., & Dasgupta, S.D. (2006). Re-examining battering: Are all acts of violence against intimate partners the same? Duluth, MN: Praxis International. Retrieved December 8, 2006, from http://www.praxisinternational.org/pages/library/files/pdf/ ReexaminingBattering.pdf.

Peterson, R.R. (2008). Reducing intimate partner violence: Moving beyond criminal justice interventions. *Criminology & Public Policy*, 7, 537–45.

Pitts, V. L., & Schwartz, M.D. (1993). Promoting self-blame among hidden rape survivors. *Humanity & Society*, 17, 383–98.

Polk, K. (2003). Masculinities, femininities, and homicide: Competing explanations for male violence. In M.D. Schwartz & S.E. Hatty (Eds.), *Controversies in critical criminology* (pp. 133–46). Cincinnati: Anderson.

Porter, T. (2006). *Becoming part of the solution*. New York: A Call to Men: National Association of Men and Women Committed to Ending Violence Against Women.

Pottie Bunge, V. (2002). National trends in intimate partner homicides, 1974–2000. *Juristat*, 22. Ottawa: Statistics Canada.

Bibliography

Powell, B., & Brown, L. (2007). 8 boys charged with sex assault on school grounds: 12- and 13-year-old students accused of restraining and groping girls; parents fear charges overblown. *Toronto Star*, October 5, A1, A27.

Price, E.L., Byers, S.E., Sears, H.A., Whelan, J., & Saint Pierre, M. (2000). *Dating violence amongst New Brunswick adolescents: A summary of two studies*. Fredericton, NB: Muriel McQueen Fergusson Centre for Family Violence Research, University of New Brunswick.

Proudfoot, S. (2009a). "Honor killings" of females on rise in Canada: Expert. *The Star Phoenix*, July 23, 1.

Proudfoot, S. (2009b). More women in shelters, many fleeing abuse: StatsCan. *CanWest News Service*, May 13, 14.

Pruitt, L.R. (2008). Place matters: Domestic violence and rural difference. *Wisconsin Journal of Law, Gender, & Society*, 23, 347–416.

Purdon, C. (2003). *Woman abuse and Ontario Works in a rural community: Rural women speak out about their experiences with Ontario Works*. Ottawa: Status of Women Canada.

R. v. Lavallee. (1990). 1 S.C.R. 852–900.

Raj, A., Silverman, J.G., Wingood, G.M., & DiClemente, R.J. (1999). Prevalence and correlates of relationship abuse among a community-based sample of low-income African-American women. *Violence Against Women*, 5, 279–91.

Ranson, G. (2009). Unpaid work: How do families divide their labour? In M. Baker (Ed.), *Families: Changing trends in Canada* (pp. 108–29). Whitby, ON: McGraw-Hill Ryerson.

Raphael, J. (2000). *Saving Bernice: Battered women, welfare, and poverty*. Boston: Northeastern University Press.

Raphael, J. (2001a). Domestic violence as a welfare-to-work barrier: Research and theoretical issues. In C.M. Renzetti, J.L. Edleson, & R.K. Bergen (Eds.), *Sourcebook on violence against women* (pp. 443–56). Thousand Oaks, CA: Sage.

Raphael, J. (2001b). Public housing and domestic violence. *Violence Against Women*, 7, 699–706.

Rathjen, H., & Montpetit, C. (1999). *December 6: From the Montreal massacre to gun control*. Toronto: McClelland & Stewart.

Reiman, J., & Leighton, P. (2010). *The rich get richer and the poor get prison: Ideology, class, and criminal justice*, 9th ed. Boston: Allyn & Bacon.

Rennison, C.M., & Welchans, S. (2000). Intimate partner violence. Washington, DC: US Department of Justice.

Renzetti, C.M. (1992). *Intimate betrayal: Partner abuse in lesbian relationships*. Newbury Park, CA: Sage.

Renzetti, C.M. (1997). Foreword. In W.S. DeKeseredy & L. MacLeod, *Woman Abuse: A sociological story* (pp. v–vii). Toronto: Harcourt Brace.

Ristock, J.L. (2002). *No more secrets: Violence in lesbian relationships*. New York: Routledge.

Romito, P. (2008). *A deafening silence: Hidden violence against women and children*. Bristol, UK: Polity Press.

Rosen, L.N., Dragiewicz, M., & Gibbs, J.C. (2009). Fathers' rights groups: Demographic correlates and impact on custody policy. *Violence Against Women*, 15, 513–31.

Rushowy, K. (2008). Hate laws: Protection for females demanded. *Toronto Star*, March 5, A19.

Russell, D.E.H. (1990). *Rape in marriage.* Expanded and revised edition. New York: Macmillan Press.

Russell, D.E.H. (1998). *Dangerous relationships: Pornography, misogyny, and rape.* Thousand Oaks, CA: Sage.

Russell, D.E.H. (2001). Femicide: Some men's "final solution" for women. In D.E.H. Russell & R.A. Harmes (Eds.), *Femicide in global perspective* (pp. 176–88). New York: Teachers College Press.

Russo, N.E. (1985). *A woman's mental health agenda.* Washington, DC: American Psychological Association.

Saltzman, L.E., Fanslow, J.L., McMahon, P.M., & Shelly, G.A. (1999). *Uniform definitions and recommended data elements for intimate partner violence surveillance.* Atlanta: National Center for Injury Prevention and Control, Centers for Disease Control and Prevention, 1999.

Sampson, R.J., Raudenbush, S.W., & Earls, F. (1998). *Neighborhood collective efficacy: Does it help reduce violence?* Washington, DC: US Department of Justice.

Sanday, P.R. (1990). *Fraternity gang rape.* New York: New York University Press.

Sauvé, J., & Burns, M. (2009). *Residents of Canada's shelters for abused women, 2008.* Ottawa: Statistics Canada.

Schissel, B. (1997). *Blaming children: Youth crime, moral panics, and the politics of hate.* Halifax: Fernwood.

Schur, E.M. (1984). *Labeling women deviant: Gender, stigma, and social control.* Philadelphia: Temple University Press.

Schwartz, M.D. (1987). Censorship of sexual violence: Is the problem sex or violence? *Humanity & Society*, 11, 212–43.

Schwartz, M.D. (2000). Methodological issues in the use of survey data for measuring and characterizing violence against women. *Violence Against Women*, 8, 815–38.

Schwartz, M.D., & DeKeseredy, W.S. (1993). The return of the "battered husband syndrome" through the typification of women as violent. *Crime, Law and Social Change*, 20, 249–65.

Schwartz, M.D., & DeKeseredy, W.S. (1994). People without data attacking rape: The Gilbertizing of Mary Koss. *Violence Update*, 5, 5, 8, 11.

Schwartz, M.D., & DeKeseredy, W.S. (1997). *Sexual assault on the college campus: The role of male peer support*. Thousand Oaks, CA: Sage.

Schwartz, M.D., & DeKeseredy, W.S. (2008). Interpersonal violence against women. *Journal of Contemporary Criminal Justice*, 24, 178–85.

Schwartz, M.D., DeKeseredy, W.S., Tait, D., & Alvi, S. (2001). Male peer support and routine activities theory: Understanding sexual assault on the college campus. *Justice Quarterly*, 18, 701–27.

Sev'er, A. (2002). *Fleeing the house of horrors: Women who have left abusive partners*. Toronto: University of Toronto Press.

Sev'er, A. (2008). Discarded daughters: The patriarchal grip, dowry deaths, sex ratio imbalances, and foeticide in India. *Women's Health and Urban Life*, 7, 56–75.

Sheehy, E.A. (2002). Legal responses to violence against women in Canada. In K.M.J. McKenna & J. Larkin (Eds.), *Violence against women: New Canadian perspectives* (pp. 473–92). Toronto: Ianna.

Shepard, M.F., & Pence, E.L. (Eds.). (1999). *Coordinating community responses to domestic violence: Lessons from Duluth and beyond*. Thousand Oaks, CA: Sage.

Sherman, L., & Berk, R. (1984). The specific deterrent effects of arrest for domestic assault. *American Sociological Review*, 49, 261–72.

Shoener, S.J. (2008). Health consequences of intimate partner violence. In C.M. Renzetti & J.L. Edleson (Eds.), *Encyclopedia of interpersonal violence*, Vol. 1 (pp. 326–27). Thousand Oaks, CA: Sage.

Silvestri, M., & Crowther-Dowey, C. (2008). *Gender and crime*. London: Sage.

Simpson, J. (2000). *Star-spangled Canadians: Canadians living the American dream*. Toronto: HarperCollins.

Sluser, R., & Kaufman, M. (1992). The White Ribbon Campaign: Mobilizing men to take action. Paper presented at the 17th National Conference on Men and Masculinity, Chicago.

Smith, M.D. (1987). The incidence and prevalence of woman abuse in Toronto. *Violence and Victims*, 2, 173–87.

Smith, M.D. (1988). *Violence and sport*. Toronto: Canadian Scholars' Press.

Smith, M.D. (1990). Patriarchal ideology and wife beating: A test of a feminist hypothesis. *Violence and Victims*, 5, 257–73.

Smith, M.D. (1994). Enhancing the quality of survey data on violence against women: A feminist approach. *Gender and Society*, 8, 109–27.

Sokoloff, N.J., & Dupont, I. (2005). Domestic violence at the intersections of race, class, and gender. *Violence Against Women*, 11, 38–64.

Stanko, E.A. (1985). *Intimate intrusions: Women's experiences of male violence*. London: Routledge & Kegan Paul.

Stanko, E.A. (1990). *Everyday violence: How women and men experience sexual and physical danger*. London: Pandora.

Stanko, E.A. (1997). Should I stay or should I go: Some thoughts on variants of intimate violence. *Violence Against Women*, 3, 629–35.

Stark, E. (2006). Commentary on Johnson's conflict and control: Gender symmetry and asymmetry in domestic violence. *Violence Against Women*, 12, 1019–1025.

Stark, E. (2007). *Coercive control: How men entrap women in personal life*. New York: Oxford University Press.

Statistics Canada. (2002). Family violence: Impacts and consequences of spousal violence. *The Daily*. Retrieved from www.statcan.ca/daily-quotidien/020626/dq020626a-eng.htm.

Statistics Canada. (2010). Study: Projections of the diversity of the Canadian population. *The Daily*, March 9, 1–4.

Steinmetz, S. (1977–78). The battered husband syndrome. *Victimology*, 3–4, 499–509.

Stout, K.D. (2001). Intimate femicide: A national demographic overview. In D.E.H. Russell & R.A. Harmes (Eds.), *Femicide in global perspective* (pp. 41–49). New York: Teachers College Press.

Straus, M.A. (1979). Measuring intrafamily conflict and violence: The Conflict Tactics (CT) Scales. *Journal of Marriage and the Family*, 41, 75–88.

Straus, M.A. (1993). Physical assaults by women: A major problem. In R.J. Gelles & D.R. Loseke (Eds.), *Current controversies on family violence* (pp. 67–87). Thousand Oaks, CA: Sage.

Straus, M.A., Gelles, R.J., & Steinmetz, S.K. (1981). *Behind closed doors: Violence in the American family*. New York: Anchor.

Straus, M.A, Hamby, S., Boney-McCoy, S., & Sugarman, D. (1996). The revised Conflict Tactics Scales (CTS2): Development and preliminary psychometric data. *Journal of Family Issues*, 17, 283–316.

Bibliography

Swan, S.C., & Snow, D.L. (2006). The development of a theory of women's use of violence in intimate relationships. *Violence Against Women*, 12, 1026–1045.

Thorne-Finch, R. (1992). *Ending the silence: The origins and treatment of male violence against women.* Toronto: University of Toronto Press.

Thornhill, R., & Palmer, C.T. (2000). *A natural history of rape: Biological bases of sexual coercion.* Boston: MIT Press.

Tjaden, P., & Thoennes, N. (2000). *Extent, nature, and consequences of intimate partner violence: Findings from the National Violence Against Women Survey.* Washington, DC: US Department of Justice.

Tolman, R.M., & Bennett, L.W. (1990). A review of quantitative research on men who batter. *Journal of Interpersonal Violence*, 5, 87–118.

Toughill, K. (2007). StatsCan confirms: Small-town folks nicer. *Toronto Star*, June 9, 6.

Tower, C.C. (2002). *Understanding child abuse and neglect.* Boston: Allyn & Bacon.

United Nations. (1993). *Strategies for confronting domestic violence: A resource manual.* New York: United Nations.

United Nations. (1995). *Focus on women: Violence against women.* Report prepared for the Fourth World Conference on Women, Action for Equality, Development and Peace. Beijing: United Nations.

Vallée, B. (2007). *The war on women: Elly Armour, Jane Hurshman, and criminal violence in Canadian homes.* Toronto: Key Porter Books.

Van Alphen, T. (2009). Busted GM to get $9.5B from Canadians. *Toronto Star*, June 1, A1, A5.

Wacquant, L.J.D. (1997). Three pernicious premises in the study of the American ghetto. *International Journal of Urban and Regional Research*, July, 341–53.

Walby, S., & Myhill, A. (2001). New survey methodologies in researching violence against women. *British Journal of Criminology*, 41, 502–22.

Walker, L. (1979). *The battered woman.* New York: Harper & Row.

Walker, S. (1998). *Sense and nonsense about crime and drugs: A policy guide*, 4th ed. Belmont, CA: West/Wadsworth.

Warr, M. (2002). *Companions in crime: The social aspects of criminal conduct.* New York: Cambridge University Press.

Warshaw, R. (1988). *I never called it rape.* New York: Harper & Row.

Watts, C., & Zimmerman, C. (2002). Violence against women: Global scope and magnitude. *The Lancet*, April 6, 359.

Websdale, N. (1998). *Rural woman battering and the justice system: An ethnography*. Thousand Oaks, CA: Sage.

Weitzer, R., & Kubrin, C.E. (2009). Misogyny in rap music: A content analysis of prevalence and meanings. *Men and Masculinities*, 12, 3–29.

Wellstone, P.D., & Wellstone, S. (2001). Foreword. In C.M. Renzetti, J.L. Edleson, & R.K. Bergen (Eds.), *Sourcebook on violence against women* (pp. ix–x). Thousand Oaks, CA: Sage.

Wilson, M., & Daly, M. (1994). *Spousal homicide*. Ottawa: Canadian Centre for Justice Statistics.

Wilson, W.J. (1996). *When work disappears: The world of the new urban poor*. New York: Knopf.

Yodanis, C.L., & Godenzi, A. (1999). *Report on the economic costs of violence against women*. Fribourg, Switzerland: Department of Social Work and Social Policy, University of Fribourg.

Zerbisias, A. (2008). Packaging abuse of women as entertainment for adults: Cruel, degrading scenes "normalized" for generation brought up in dot-com world. *Toronto Star*, January 26, L3.

Zilbergeld, B. (1983). *The shrinking of America: Myths of psychological change*. Boston: Little Brown.

Zorza, J. (2002). Domestic violence in rural America. In J. Zorza (Ed.), *Violence against women: Vol. 1: Law, prevention, protection, enforcement, treatment, and health* (pp. 14-1–14–2). Kingston, NJ: Civic Research Institute.

Index

Index

Benson, Rita, 99
Berman, Helene, "Overcoming Violence in the Lives of Girls and Young Women," 63
Bernardo, Paul, 52
Bertuzzi, Todd, 2
Bowker, Lee, 69
bullying, 102
Bunch, Ted, 114
Bush, George W., 18, 20–21

Calgary Women's Emergency Shelter, 77
A Call to Men Committed to Ending Violence Against Women, 114
Canada, 61
 crime-control policies, 18. *See also* criminal justice policies; police
 gender inequality, 72
 intimate femicide in, 21–25
 living standard, 17
 measurable health-related economic costs of violence against women, 95
 as a non-violent country, 39
 ongoing systemic violence against women, 25
 perceived as safer than US, 17
 percentage of beaten women who leave partners, 77
 social safety net cuts, 121
 stranger-to-stranger murders, 18
Canada the "peaceable kingdom" cliché, 17
Canadian Criminal Code, 6
Canadian Feminist Alliance for International Action (CFAFIA), 87
Canadian National Survey of Woman Abuse in University/College Dating (CNS), 5–6, 12, 28–29, 35, 37, 66, 69, 73
Canadian Panel on Violence Against Women, 112
Canadian Police Information Centre (CPIC), 111
Canadian spanking laws, 2
Cancer, 3
Caringella, Susan, 110, 112
censorship, 113, 124
Centers for Disease Control and Prevention in Atlanta, 14
Chapman, Jane, 99

Chicago Women's Health Risk Study, 33
child care, 88, 91, 122
child custody and access issues, 78–79, 89–90
child participation in creation and implementation of policies, 55
child pornography, 64–65
children
 Canadian youth access to pornography, 64
 dating victimization (elementary school), 35
 death of unborn child, 23, 74
 infant mortality rates, 56
 malnourishment of, 56
 physical abuse of girls by boys, 31
 physical childhood abuse risk factor for cancer, 3
 powerless under Canadian and US laws, 55
 progressive child activists, 55
 sexual assaults (12- and 13-year-olds in schoolyard incident), 7–8
 spanking, 2–3
children who have witnessed woman abuse, 93, 95, 98–102
 resources for, 78
Christenssen, Ferrel, 50
citizen concern about controlling crime
 Canada *vs.* US, 18
Clean Hotel Initiative, 113
Cobb, Chris, 51
Cocelli, Turan, 23
Cohen, Stanley, 54
collective efficacy, absence of, 89–91
Collins, Patricia Hill, 124
colonialism, 13
"community backlash" response to victimization, 32
community visits, 89
community-based approaches to helping the abused, 78
Conflict Tactics Scale (CTS), 6, 44–45, 56
 ideological and factual assumptions behind, 46
 measures only conflict-instigated violence, 49

problematic interpretations of,
47–49, 51
as reliable method of eliciting sensitive data, 46
Conflict Tactics Scale 2 (CTS2), 49–50
Conlin, Tanya, *After She Leaves,* 99
Connell, Bob, 35
Conservative government. *See* Harper
government
Corry, John, *A Satirical View of London
at the Commencement of the Nineteenth Century,* 22
Creba, Jane, 18
crime surveys, 6–7
crime victim, meaning of term, 1–2
Criminal Harassment/Anti-Stalking
Law (1993), 78
criminal justice policies
Canada *vs.* US, 18
need for dedicated police unit for
woman assault, 111
zero tolerance policy, 106
criminal justice reform recommenda-
tions, 110–11
criminal justice system, 105–11, 117. *See
also* family court system
arrests and charges, 7–8, 77, 106–9
counter-charges against the woman,
106–7
disempowerment of battered
women, 107
effectiveness in protecting women,
108–9, 126
legal aid, 87–88, 122
only one part of the solution, 126
symbolic functions (send message to
male abusers), 109
Cross, Pamela, 21–22
Currie, Elliott, 55, 109
cyber sexual assaults, 27–28

Darwinian thought, 55
Dasgupta, S.D., 57
date rape, 21, 95–96. *See also* sexual assaults in university/college dating
relationships
dating victimization, 35
Day, Tanis, 95
definitions of violence against women
broad definitions, 9, 12, 16

definition differences due to disciplines, 14–15
effect on how data is gathered, 5
effect on social support services, 5
narrow definitions, 5–9
use as tools in social struggles, 5
degradation ceremonies, 59
DeKeseredy, Walter S., 58, 82–83
depression, 36, 83
diversity issues, 123. *See also* Aboriginal
women; immigrant and refugee
women across Canada
domestic homicides. *See also* femicide;
spousal homicides
majority precipitated by male
violence, 23
domestic homicides (1995–2004)
one-third of solved murders in
Canada, 23
domestic violence. *See also* violence
against women
health effects of, 40
not gender-neutral social problem,
24
Domestic Violence Action Plan
(Ontario), 97
Domestic Violence Death Review Committee (Ontario, 2002–2005), 24
Donnermeyer, Joseph, 84
Dragiewicz, Molly, 19
Durham Region study, 88–89
Dutton, Donald, 7, 47, 49, 51, 57, 60

École Polytechnique massacre, 13,
102, 118
economic abuse, 5, 11, 43, 89
economic reasons for staying or
returning, 86–88, 91
economic reforms, 119–21
economically disadvantaged women.
See women who are poor
Ehrenreich, Barbara, 120
elderly women, 13
elementary-school students
dating victimization, 35
Elias, Robert, 1
Elizabeth Fry Society, 85
Ellard, Kelly, 53
emotional abuse. *See* psychological
abuse
emotional separation

Index

viewed as "soft-core abuse," 6
web of emotional abuse, 80–83
psychological and emotional abuse.
See psychological abuse
psychological programs for violent
men in Canada, 61–62, 78
psychological theories explaining
violence, 60–61. *See also* mental
illness
"psychologizing and decriminalizing"
violence against women, 62
Ptotenhauer, Nancy, 19–20
public awareness campaigns, 112
public degradation ceremonies, 43
public housing, living in
as predictor of violence against
women, 36
public transportation, 122
absence of in rural areas, 86

Quality of Neighbourhood Life
Survey, 38

racism, 27, 82, 111
rap music, 124
rape crisis/sexual assault centres in
Canada
financial costs, 97
rape drugs, 56
rape survivors, 9
"RapeLay" video game, 67
Raphael, Jody, 120
Reena Virk murder, 53
media coverage, 52
"regretted sex," 27
Renzetti, Claire, 110
restraining orders, 111
retirement ages, 121
Ricci, Christina, 54
road rage, 56
rural communities
patriarchy, 90
special needs in, 122
stereotypical gender roles, 86
violent men protected by "ol' boys
network," 86
rural crime, 83–84
rural Ohio separation/divorce sexual
assault study, 9, 11, 24, 31, 59, 66, 69,
73, 88–89, 93, 98

male peers legitimated woman
abuse, 90
rural women, 83
abuse seldom reported, 86
lack of economic opportunity, 86
police may be friends with abusers,
86
similar rates of violence to urban
women, 84
Russell, Diana E.H., 10, 33, 64, 68
Rust, Kevin, 47

sabotaging work efforts. *See also*
stalking
influencing employers to fire
women, 88
Saltzman, Linda, 14
Sanday, Peggy Reeves, 68
*A Satirical View of London at the
Commencement of the Nineteenth
Century* (Corry), 22
school shootings, 56
school-aged children
dating victimization, 35
effects of woman abuse on, 100
Schur, Edwin, 6
Schwartz, Martin, 4, 9, 44, 58, 69, 95
See Jane Hit (Garbarino), 53
self-defence, 48, 50
sensational cases of female violence,
51–54
separated and divorced women, 31
financial problems, 88
higher risk of intimate violence,
24, 38
most at risk for intimate femicide,
33, 78
sexual assault, 9, 70, 74
still at risk from patriarchal men, 74
separation. *See also* leaving abusive
relationships
risk factor for femicide, 23–24, 33, 78
as solution to problem of wife
abuse, 33, 74
as tactical manoeuvre that carries a
calculated risk, 79–80
victim's *vs.* outsiders' expectations, 79
separation/divorce assault, 6, 19, 49, 73
status among peers and, 70
serial and mass killers, 52, 54, 102–3
Sesen, Aysun (and unborn child), 23

Index

Violence Against Women (journal), 4, 57, 110

Violence Against Women Act (VAWA) (US), 19–20

Violence Against Women classes, 25

violence in intimate heterosexual relationships. *See* intimate partner violence

violence in US TV shows, 18

violence-related stress, 96

Virk, Reena, 52–53

visible minority women, 31, 38

Voices of our Sisters in the Spirit, 85

war on women, 22, 102

warning signs of woman abuse (table), 116

Warr, Mark, 69

Warshaw, Robin, 116

web of emotional abuse, 80–83

Websdale, Neil, 90

well-meaning men, 114

When She Was Bad (Pearson), 51

White Ribbon Campaign, 118

white supremacy, 66

"wife only working" family, 36

without delay response to violence against women calls, 111

woman abuse, 4, 79. *See also* sexual assaults; violence against women

arrests and charges, 32, 80, 106, 108

awareness about, 77, 111

financial consequences, 96–98

impact on children, 93, 95, 98–102

major public health problem, 40, 95

as medical or psychiatric problem, 60, 78. *See also* mental illness

men who gain from, 119

physical health consequences, 94

pressure from community to accept, 82

psychological consequences, 95–96

tolerance of, 89

as violation of women's human rights, 125–26

warning signs (table), 116

widespread acceptance of, 32, 82, 89

women's behaviour and, 44, 60

women are as violent as men argument, 6, 19, 47, 51, 58

women from minority cultures, 123. *See also* Aboriginal women; immigrant and refugee women across Canada; visible minority women

women in urban public housing, 31

women "twice victimized," 20

women who are excluded from mainstream surveys, 39–40

women who are poor

higher risk of physical assault, 38

risk of sexual assault, 31

women with disabilities, 13, 40, 88

women with special needs, 122–23

women's and girls' use of violence, 5, 43–58

atypical examples, 52–53

feminist researchers on, 57

in movies, 53

women's groups. *See also* feminists

emphasis on partnership and collaboration, 112

women's increased labour-force participation, 37

women's shelters, 22, 77–78, 81, 97

women's studies, 12–13

"Women's Use of Violence in Intimate Relationships," 57

work hardening, 120

work week, 121

World Health Organization, 40

Wuornos, Aileen, 54

Youth Criminal Justice Act, 8

YWCA Canada, 21

zero tolerance policy, 106